CHRONICLES OF A STAND-UP GUY

A Peek into the Daily Grind of a Comedian

MICKEY HOUSLEY

Chasing Kites
publishing

SCHOOL

Now It's Your Turn

Discover the EXACT 3-step blueprint you need to become
a bestselling author in 3 months.
Self-Publishing School helped me, and now I want
them to help you with this FREE WEBINAR!
Even if you're busy, bad at writing, or don't know
where to start,
you CAN write a bestseller and build your
best life.

With tools and experience across a variety niches
and professions,
Self-Publishing School is the <u>only</u> resource you
need to
take your book to the finish line!

DON'T WAIT

**Watch this FREE WEBINAR now, and
Say "YES" to becoming a bestseller:**

I dedicate this book to my entire family, who has shown me nothing but love and support ever since I began the journey of standup comedy.

To my parents, who have nurtured me from birth well into adulthood and heavily influence my sense of humor and kindness.

To my brothers Dion, Dejuan, and Denzell, and my sister Mariah, who have each helped me become the man and comedian I am today through sibling love and rivalry.

To my wife Sandrell, whose great sacrifices helped make the completion of this book possible. And to her family, who have become some of my biggest cheerleaders.

Contents

Introduction

Hey! Mickey Housley here. I am a professional comedian of nine years. In other words, this is what I do. Through comedy I've been able to travel the country, perform with guys I watched on TV as a child, and my personal favorite —put gas in my car.

Standup comedy is the best job in the world. However, it's not the easiest. To enjoy the fruits that standup comedy has to offer, one must be able to persevere. It's much like becoming a doctor. You may put in 7–10 years of practice —eating noodles the entire time—before you're able to establish a career. It's tough, but the code in comedy is, "Once you start, you can't quit."

From a fan's perspective, seeing an artist evolve is one of the coolest things about entertainment. We love watching the growth of the actress from her first movie to the next movie and beyond. Talk to someone who's seen a band perform before the fame and they'll speak with a certain fondness.

"I saw little known Maroon 5 open for Destiny's Child when I was fifteen. I always knew those kids would be something."

I hear it about comedians all the time.

"Man, I remember when so and so first started. He was horrible, but I told him to keep at it. That boy is good now!"

Maybe you don't know any comedians that struggled in the beginning. Well, now you do! In the pages that follow, I'll take you on my journey to becoming funny on stage and establishing a career as a full-time comedian. If you're a comedy fan looking for someone new to root for, I invite you on this journey. When we're done, feel free to email me at mickeyhousley@gmail.com and tell me to "keep at it!"

Perhaps you're a young comedian hoping to learn a few Dos and Don'ts of the comedy game. Well, I've done plenty of Don'ts and I share them all. I invite you on this journey as I share the highs and lows that standup comedy offers!

When people meet comedians they usually want to know how we got started in comedy. For me, the quest began on...

March 18, 2005, I hosted the talent show at Sharpstown High School. Unbeknownst to me at the time, I was stepping into the world of standup comedy. I did something that afternoon that I would do hundreds of times more in the future—make people laugh and enjoy the high.

Perhaps God had a plan for me to be a comedian all along and this was His way of introducing me to the art form. Still, I wasn't thinking about becoming a comedian at the time. I was just being me, and it worked out great. Standup was four years away, and two significant events needed to take place.

First, in the summer of 2008, Miesha, a friend from high school, invited me to a gathering that one of her aunts was holding at her house. While there, Miesha introduced me to her older cousin Kena Monique, founder of Kena Monique Entertainment. This was my first formal introduction to Kena, but I already knew who she was. She produced comedy shows in large venues all around Houston, starring nationally-known comedians such as Cedric the Entertainer, Monique and D.L. Hughley. Additionally, Kena's husband, Sir Michael Tiggs, was my football coach at Sharpstown.

I was at the gathering having a good time and making the house guests laugh. Kena took notice and suggested I become a comedian. I heard this often, but I always took it as merely a compliment for saying or doing something silly. I never saw comedy as a realistic dream.

All that changed one day when my dad dragged me to a bar to perform karaoke with him. He had been urging me to try it for months, but I thought karaoke was something that only girls did. I finally agreed to go with him after feeling guilty over wrecking his car. He nudged me at just the right time, and I ended up loving it. Needless to say, I've been hooked ever since.

While my singing on a good day could cause trauma to any

ear caught off guard, I did have a penchant for entertaining. People found me hysterical, and on many occasions I would exit the stage to standing ovations. (I once had an entire club chanting my name.) For the first time since high school, when I stood on the karaoke stage, I had an audience.

Then I saw Charles. Charles was an older gentleman that sang at the same karaoke bars as me. One night he was granted permission from Hump Dogg, the karaoke jockey at Legends Grill, to perform standup. Charles wasn't very good, but he had one joke about getting drunk that lit up the room. I was sitting just a few feet from Charles as he performed his routine and seeing him get that big laugh gave me a jolt of courage.

"I can do that!"

Before long I began writing jokes. And not long after—a journal.

A Journey Begins

FEBRUARY 24, 2009

A COUPLE OF WEEKS AGO, I finally decided to put any doubts aside and pursue a career as a comedian. So far I've been writing material, but I need to rehearse what I'm writing. I am going under the moniker Mick Bizzy, and I want to be one of the GREATS! The world will most certainly know my real name, but for now I want something that catches people's attention.

I never performed as Mick Bizzy. I first took the stage as simply Mickey. I soon added my middle name and went by Mickey Devon, but that sounded more like an R&B singer than a comedian. By the end of the year, I changed it and became the man you now know as Mickey Housley.

FEBRUARY 25, 2009

I WAS PULLED over the other day, but by the grace of God I wasn't taken to jail. Because I have a suspended driver's license there was a possibility I could've spent a couple of weeks in downtown Houston. The only thing I could think about during the stop was all the time I'd be missing writing material. It motivated me to focus more. Right now, I must learn to stick to my game plan and not let daily distractions like basketball deter me.

FEBRUARY 27, 2009

FOR THE SECOND time in three days I got pulled over. This time my mother was with me, and thanks to her the officer gave us a break. It turned out to be the best thing that happened to me in my early comic career. It forced me to stay at my mom's house for a while. Feeling bored, I decided to walk the neighborhood. While doing so, I discovered a comfortable way of rehearsing my material. This was the day I came up with the concept for my first show.

Being a black man with tinted windows can be tricky. If I leave the windows up, I get a ticket for dark windows. If I roll the windows down, I get a ticket for dark skin. #loselosesituation

MARCH 8, 2009

I HELPED my grandpa Joe with his yard work today. I didn't want to, but how can I say no to grandpa? He enjoys watching his grandsons tend to his yard. He'll literally sit on his porch with a glass of juice with his face focused on our work as if he's coaching a football game.

After I finished the chores, I found time to research the careers of great comedians. Reading about guys like Chris Rock, Rodney Dangerfield, and Sam Kinison further inspired me.

I'm also reading *How Can I Get Myself to Do What I Need to Do* by Terry Gogna. It has taught me the power of implanting powerful and positive affirmations into my subconscious mind.

MARCH 10, 2009

I WAS TALKING to an intern doctor yesterday, and he was telling me how he was able to work with experienced doctors by reaching out and simply asking to work and learn from them. I felt I should surely do the same as a comic. I should be able to approach a veteran comedian and see if it'd be okay to pick his or her brain.

Speaking of which, I logged in to Myspace today and reached out to Kena Monique to see about networking. I told her that I did not forget what she told me last summer and I've decided I want to be a comedian. She happily responded and told me about a venue called Smokey's that does comedy on Thursday nights.

MARCH 11, 2009

I WATCHED an ESPN special on NBA All-Star Kevin Garnett earlier, and I became really motivated by his work ethic. By the time the show ended I began looking up comedy clubs on the internet. I called the Laff Stop and they told me they have open mic on Wednesdays. Perfect! My original plan was to have my first performance on Friday at Legends Grill like Charles did. However, I think tonight will serve as better practice and exposure for me.

MARCH 13, 2009

I NEED TO WORK HARDER, be more confident and stop giving in to sleep. I need to treat this like my business. I didn't get to perform at the Laff Stop the other night because I was late. So far that was my first true lesson in my journey to comic greatness. I was depending on other people to get me to the show when I should've just been more responsible. But it's okay, for today I'm a stronger person and a better comedian.

MARCH 21, 2009

WEDNESDAY AND THURSDAY were breakthrough days for me. I performed standup comedy for the first time at The Laff Stop on Wednesday and at Smokey's on Thursday. I would have to say I did fair at both locations. I got enough laughs to feed my confidence. I can do this. I used the same material both times talking about how females always hit guys with the "let's just be friends" line.

My brothers, Dejuan and Denzell, came with me to the shows along with a few friends, which was cool. My grandma Beulah came to the show at Smokey's where a comedian named Eddie B playfully roasted her for wearing all green.

Looking back at my writings, I'm surprised I didn't provide more detail of my first performance, neither did I seem particularly excited about it, and trust me I was. My first notepad was small, and I kept all my entries confined to one page at the time so that probably best explains why I didn't go into much detail on the first two shows.

MARCH 28, 2009

ANOTHER VENUE that Kena recommended I perform at was Tyme Square. This past Wednesday I was able to perform there for the first time. I met the owner [*or so I thought at the time*], Tom Webb, and he had some encouraging words for me. He told me once I got comfortable, I presented the stage presence needed to make a normally tough crowd laugh. He was impressed and told me I could work on my material there anytime free of charge. The cover charge is usually $3.

APRIL 1, 2009

LAST NIGHT I rode with fellow comic Marcos Edwards to the Jazz It Up Cafe where they host comedy on Tuesday nights. The emcee there is a guy by the name of Adam Bob. My time there was really flattering. After embedding positive affirmations in my head, I performed with a lot more confidence on stage. I talked about how I feel that some of God's people are lazy. I would have to say that this would be my first true knockout material. There were older women calling me cute while I was onstage and told me to watch out for cougars. One of them even left me a $20 tip.

Comedians sometimes get asked, "How long did it take you to get paid doing standup?"

Well according to this entry, it took me thirteen days. Not bad. Of course, it was just a tip, albeit a generous one. Although I soon started getting booked for paid shows, it would take years before I received a tip again.

APRIL 2, 2009

YESTERDAY AT TYME SQUARE I got my first taste of how tough an audience can be. I hit them with some good material, but I was unfortunately hit back with blank stares. But it was cool because it was a learning experience. Now I know I must work harder.

During my first night at Smokey's, I met a veteran comedian by the name of Eric Bowens. He told me that in order to improve I must have my own comedy room. So today I'll be going to some bars to see if I can host a comedy night. Also, later I'll be hooking up with Eric at his home to learn the comedy game a bit more.

My first two weeks doing standup were fun. Every time you step on stage it's a win regardless of what happens, and that first performance was a huge win. I met some cool comics, and Eric Bowens served as an early mentor. I obliged when he suggested I start a comedy night. However, he was stunned at how quickly I would make that happen.

2

A Legend in the Making

APRIL 4, 2009

FOR THE PAST eight months I've been doing karaoke on Wednesdays and Fridays at Legends Bar & Grill. I sometimes thought this was an unproductive activity and I should slow down on the karaoke. Apparently, I was wrong. When you faithfully support a place of business, the owner supports you. This proved to be true yesterday as Legends' owner, Xavier, agreed to let me host open mic comedy at his club on Sundays. What a blessing!

APRIL 9, 2009

YESTERDAY I TOOK part in my first competition. I found out about it the day of as Kena called and encouraged me to give it a go. I believe I did OK, but my goal was to walk off stage knowing I did great. The first round was judged by the audience, and I was probably in the bottom half in terms of applauds given. The event was held at Diallo's of Houston and hosted by Magic 102.1's Kandi Eastman. The winners were comedians Blame the Comic and Eric Bowens. They won the chance to open for an upcoming show this weekend starring Arnez J, Sommore, and Earthquake.

APRIL 13, 2009

THE PATH to comic greatness has brought me closer to God because I know that my success is not my doing but His. So daily I'm fighting the temptation of a certain sin because I don't want to mess up the gift God has blessed me with. In fact, I will be fasting from food sometime soon so that I may get closer to God and stay focused on Him. My prayer is that He blesses my family as well as my career.

> But seek first the kingdom of God and His
> righteousness, and all these things will
> be provided for you ~
>
> Matthew 6:33

APRIL 18, 2009

TOMORROW IS THE BIG DAY. It's the first day Legends Bar & Grill will showcase open mic comedy. It will be hosted by none other than *Me*. Today I must get on the computer at my grandma Zona's house and promote like crazy. Tomorrow is going to be huge. Unfortunately, I have to compete with the NBA playoffs which start today, as well as this rain that has come out of nowhere.

APRIL 20, 2009

SO LAST NIGHT I hosted my own comedy room for the first time. It was an interesting experience. I would have to say it was successful in several ways. The audience showed up and thanks to Eric Bowens so did the comics (although late). He brought out Kier "Junior" Spates, Black Prince, and Terry "The Grossman" Gross among others. Terry and my dad realized they knew each other and used to work together for Gallery Furniture. I found that rather cool.

Although the show was great, I know I must increase the promotion to maintain a decent-sized audience. I learned that I need to manage the show a little better in terms of what I allow the comics to do and how long they perform. The thing that disappointed me most was that I didn't insert enough of my set in the show. Something I need to work on.

APRIL 22, 2009

SO I finally got to hook up with Eric Bowens after a couple of failed attempts. He's a real cool dude who has a strong desire and hunger to be one of the best. Learning from him at his house was my first time witnessing a comedian's work ethic off stage. We viewed some videos of his performances at the Houston Improv and Gotham Comedy Club in New York. We also worked on ways to promote the room I started at Legends. He was quite impressed that I started a comedy room immediately after he suggested I do so.

I got the most out of the night when he put in a documentary DVD of Jerry Seinfeld. The video had so much hard work illustrated in it, which really expanded my mind.

That DVD was of course the popular documentary "Comedian," which partially chronicled the careers of Jerry Seinfeld and Orny Adams.

APRIL 27, 2009

LAST NIGHT WAS the second night of Open Mic Comedy at Legends Bar & Grill. My phone has been off for several days and I didn't promote as hard as I should have. It was still a nice turnout nonetheless. (Everyone was just so focused on Yao Ming and the Houston Rockets, but once the game was finished it made for a good show.)

I gained more confidence in myself and became more excited in what I do. After the show, Leroy Williams, a comedian and Hypnotist also known as the Hypnobro, gave me a few pointers to help my show. I also learned to deal with comics in a more professional manner.

MAY 15, 2009

WOW! It's been over two weeks since I last wrote in this journal. To be honest, my focus has been rather off lately. Part of the reason may have to do with this girl I met about two weeks ago. I've warned myself about dating at this stage of my life. This comedy business is real important to me so I need to be careful. I would like to have a girl, however, only if she's real and willing to go through some ups and downs with me on my path to Comic Greatness.

MAY 27, 2009

EARLIER, I went to check out the Houston's Funniest Person Competition. It's the premier comedy contest in the city. It was fun, and I got a good feel of what the audience liked. I'm confident that I'll be able to advance when I perform on June 9th. One person that I know would've advanced on the 9th is comedian Al Rhodes. However, I was sadly informed at the Laff Stop today that he had passed away. I only knew him for a month, but he was real cool and showed a lot of love.

R.I.P. Al Rhodes. Thanks for all the advice!

JUNE 2, 2009

AFTER HAVING to cancel my show at Legends for the second week in a row due to lack of comics, I decided to can the room altogether. I'll either bring it back to Legends in a couple of months or look to relocate. It was a great learning experience and I'm looking forward to doing it again in the future while working harder to ensure its success. In the meantime, I'm going to go through a rigorous work routine to make myself a better comic faster. I'm ready to take this thing more seriously.

Running a comedy show does indeed sharpen your stage performance. If you're going to perform in front of an audience each week, you better be coming up with material. My run at Legends was short lived, but it did help. When you get better at something you tend to want to see how you measure up. The best way to discover that is through some good ol' friendly competition.

3

Ready for Combat

JUNE 4, 2009

LAST NIGHT I went to Tyme Square and it was probably my best experience there so far. Due to lack of an audience, Tom Webb was tempted to cancel the show. After deciding against it, the two of us found ourselves in an epic dance contest in which he kicked by butt. The show then began, and I got to practice and learn from more experienced comics as they worked the room.

The show was special as it later served as a tribute to the late, great Houston comedian, Alfred Rhodes. Tom Webb called all the comics in the building to the stage including little ol' me. Every comic onstage was very experienced. I've only been performing for two months and didn't feel worthy to share the stage with those guys. So it felt extra good to be included in honoring Al.

JUNE 10, 2009

WELL, I got a taste of the Houston Funniest Person Competition. It was my second time performing in a competition. And for the second time I failed to advance past the first round. I felt as though I did pretty good regardless, but there were flaws in my set that better preparation could have prevented. Having to go first kind of caught me off guard, but let's not make excuses, especially since being late was the reason I had to go first. As for now, I will focus on getting better so the first round of competitions will be a cinch.

Be on time comedians!

JULY 2, 2009

THE OTHER DAY I was able to download the song "Cater 2 You" by Destiny's Child. This is great because I came up with the idea to do a dance bit imitating how I would want my girl to treat me every time I come home.

In other news, I recently learned that Kena is moving to California soon. Yesterday she had her going away party and I missed it. I feel so awful. Nevertheless, I still wish to keep in touch with her while she's in Cali. My goal is to work hard while she's gone so we can really benefit from each other.

Michael Jackson died a week before and I remember it vividly because I was in the city jail when the news broke. Mama couldn't save me that time.

JULY 4, 2009

THIS WILL PROBABLY BE the best Independence Day in my early life. I am competing in a contest called The Houston Comedy Knockout Competition. I'm excited to be able to provide entertainment to an audience on a day where people would normally be with their families or at the club. I'm far more confident about this competition than the first two I competed in. My goal is not necessarily to win but rather to just do my best and leave the building with a satisfied audience.

JULY 5, 2009

BY GOD'S DOING, not mine, I am the City of Houston's first Comedy Knockout champ. It looks like third time's a charm. After being eliminated in the first round of my first two competitions, I was able to not only advance to the second round but actually win the whole thing. The dance bit that I created to the Destiny's Child song is what pushed me over the top. I won $100 not to mention some credibility. Most importantly, it was a personal confidence booster. I'm making it a point to stay humble about the victory, but it sure feels good to accomplish this after three months in the business.

MY VICTORY *in the Houston Comedy Knockout Competition was the last thing I wrote about in my original notepad. I bought another small notepad and continued writing about my adventures in comedy. Unfortunately, the second notepad ran away from home. It wanted no part of this book and I must respect its wishes. Therefore, I'm left with a six-month gap of experiences that I can't recall off the top of my head.*

When I finished writing in notepad number two, I bought a standard-sized notebook. You'll notice from here on that the entries are a bit longer than the previous ones.

I hope this doesn't frighten you.

4

Wrapping Up the Rookie Year

JANUARY 13, 2010

I KNOW I'M LATE, but Happy New Year to all. I don't know why it took me two weeks to write my first entry of the new year, but I would like to start off by letting everyone who's a victim of the massive earthquake that hit the island of Haiti yesterday know that my heart and prayers go out to you all.

One of my best friends, Jude, is from Port Au Prince, Haiti and most of his family still live there so the news hit kind of close to home for me. I pray that his parents and siblings are okay and that he's able to hear from them soon.

Last night I performed at Club Sensation. The show is run by Comedian Toucheé Jackson. He surprised me by letting me guest host the show. I hadn't hosted a show since I canned my comedy night at Legends, but I ended up doing an exceptional job and I thanked him for the opportunity.

JANUARY 17, 2010

YESTERDAY, comedian Eddie Griffin (*Malcolm & Eddie*, *Undercover Brother*) was in town headlining a show that featured Houston Heavyweights Keisha Hunt and Ali Siddiq. I was offered a chance to enjoy the show backstage. However, I declined to go altogether.

Instead, I opted to help my friend Jude and Houston's Haitian community with the earthquake relief efforts. It really felt good to know that I'm helping to make a difference even if it's in the least bit.

Funny story about Eddie Griffin—a fellow comedian and I once asked him a question that got us both punched in the chest. It wasn't anything malicious, just his odd way of answering questions. I hope.

JANUARY 20, 2010

COMEDIAN EDDIE B put together a show he calls the Laugh Off Comedy Show. It's a monthly show that he started in October, and the shows so far have been amazing. Last night I was able to perform on the show and I had a good set. Additionally, the night proved to be interesting in a couple of ways.

First, I received the opportunity to be on one of Deva Mack's upcoming comedy shows. Deva is one of the top screenwriters in Houston. She puts on a lot of plays and sketch comedy shows in the city. Since the show is going to celebrate her birthday, all the comedians are going to get the chance to roast her. That should be fun.

Secondly, I got a chance to meet comedian Shawn Harris for the first time. He is the nephew of the late, great Robin Harris (*Bebe's Kids and House Party*). Shawn was cool and even complimented me on my set.

JANUARY 25, 2010

I PROBABLY HAD the most fun I've ever had on a show in my young comedic career this past Saturday. As I mentioned before, comedienne Deva Mack celebrated her birthday by putting on one of her awesome shows that featured standup comedy as well as skits.

This was my first time being featured on a Deva Mack show. It proved to be a wonderful experience. It was held at the Midtown Art Theater and the show was hosted by Eddie B. I was the first comic on the list. Now before I even started the show, I was faced with a challenge. For the first time in my life, I lost my voice. However, that was not going to stop me from performing in front of such a beautiful crowd.

I used my go-to material only to find modest success. Feeling that I was losing the crowd, I decided it was time to wrap up my show. I mean, after all, I could barely speak. However, suddenly the unthinkable happened.

A cute girl was walking down a small set of stairs to find a seat up front. Out of the blue, she tripped and fell using her free hand to keep from completely hitting the ground. While all the attention in the room shifted to her, my eyes shifted to the wine glass occupying her other hand that somehow managed to *not* lose a single drop of the cocktail that filled it. It was a truly remarkable feat. When I acknowledged this fact to the audience, they all gazed at the glass still elevated high in the air and went bananas!

All the other comics on the show did great, the skits were hilarious, and the whole night was just incredible. I'm sure it was a birthday Deva will remember for a long time especially since all of the comics that roasted her were so good.

Often while performing, unexpected things happen. Sometimes unexpected people happen. They can alter the show for better or worse. I routinely pray for these happenings. In a nutshell, I ask that God will provide me with material that I don't have pre-prepared. I then take the stage ready for the unexpected and He usually does provide.

A cute girl trips, a microphone stand breaks, or an old lady complains about not having any cookies. Suddenly, I have an extra five to ten minutes of funny.

Deva's birthday was the first show that I recall reciting that prayer, and I've kept at it ever since.

MARCH 3, 2010

SO LAST NIGHT I went to the Improv for the Humor for Haiti show. It was the first time I've been to the Improv since maybe November when I saw Kevin Hart perform. This time around I was privileged enough to have a date!

The show was great, however a bit too long. It featured a host of performers which included Lil Brough, Dave Lawson, and Ali Siddiq just to name a few. The show was hosted by Shawn Harris and was headlined by the African King of Comedy, Michael Blackson.

I feel like I moved a step closer to my goal of performing on the Improv stage. Every time I go, I can envision myself on that stage and I get so motivated. After the show, I ran into Shawn Harris and he told me that he wanted me on one of his shows. He didn't specify which one, but let's hope he meant the Improv.

Girls that are real pretty, but also real dumb don't make sense to me. They're foxymorons.

MARCH 8, 2010

THIS PAST WEEKEND marked the first time I performed outside of Houston. It was a learning experience to say the least. After performing on Deva Mack's birthday show, she asked me to emcee the latest play she had written.

After weeks of rehearsing with Deva Mack Productions, we were prepared to take the hit stage play *Me, You, & Your Wife: You Need to Choose* on the road to Killeen, TX. The cast gathered at Deva's house Friday to spend the night. Early Saturday morning, the fourteen-member crew along with two spouses hit the road to Killeen, six cars in all.

We arrived in Killeen at about 9:00 a.m. Showtime wasn't until 7:30 p.m. so we were in great shape. Everything went smoothly leading up to showtime. We ate, rehearsed, and promoted the show at the mall. We even had enough time to rest. Actually, I almost rested a little too long. When the limo came to pick up the cast from the hotel, everyone quickly loaded up ready to go to the venue. I, on the other hand, was fast asleep. If it wasn't for my friend Sticks knocking on my hotel room door, I would've been left behind.

Okay, now onto the real drama. We arrived at the venue around 6:30 p.m. to get dressed and prepare for the show. With me being the host, I performed for a few minutes and then I introduced the play.

The play started, and the first half appeared to run smoothly. Once the first half concluded, I went back out to announce intermission and give a shout out to the promoter and sound crew as instructed. When I gave the sound crew their shout out, someone in the audience yelled, "F*** the sound crew." This prompted me to ask, "Did somebody just say, 'f*** the sound crew?'"

I went back to the dressing room and the lead sound guy chased me down pissed that I had repeated what was said. Honestly, I couldn't blame whoever shouted the insult because there were issues with the sound, but try telling that to the sound guy. He wasn't the only one pissed either.

Before the second half started, Deva called the cast together to inform us that the promoter was upset with the amount of cursing in the show and requested his money back. His reason being that some people left the show and requested a refund because of language they found to be offensive. Deva was tempted to end the show but decided to proceed on. Contrary to what the promoter told us, the arena was still packed, and the audience enjoyed the remainder of the play.

While there were some that did indeed leave, it was because the promoter presented the show as a gospel play around the churches in Killeen to sell more tickets. So that explained why those that left were upset with the vulgar language. In the end, Deva gave the shyster all his money back and vowed to never deal with him again.

No need to worry, because bigger blessings are in store for Deva Mack Productions.

MARCH 19, 2010 (Recap)

AT AGE twenty-three and now a standup comedian, I decided to throw a comedy show for my birthday. Since I was also approaching my one-year anniversary as a comedian, I figured the celebration would be a two for one calling it MickeyLodeon Fest.

I held the event at Yum Yums where I would often go to karaoke on Friday nights. I asked the owner, Steve, if I could bring some comedian friends to perform for my birthday. So basically, it was your regularly scheduled party night at Yum Yums interrupted by roughly forty-five minutes of comedy. It worked. Steve loved it and wanted me to host a comedy show at the club on Wednesday nights. I was reluctant at first, but after more urging from Steve, I obliged.

APRIL 21, 2010 (Recap)

"IT IZ WHAT IT IZ WEDNEZDAYZ" waz born. I gave Zteve (ok I'm done). I gave Steve an original launch date of April 14th, but I flaked on it by giving him an excuse about it being my mother's birthday, which it was. The truth is, I wasn't too thrilled about starting another comedy night. I had tried my hand at it with Legends and it fizzled out rather quickly. Getting a crowd in every week proved challenging, and I was in no rush to return to that grind.

Steve was persistent, however, so I promised him that we would launch the following Wednesday. Fridays and Saturdays were very busy nights at Yum Yums so I made a point to hang out both nights to mingle with folks and promote the show. The work paid off because the first official comedy night at Yum Yums was a smashing success.

A short while after, and after a legendary run of eleven years, Tom Webb ended his Wednesday night room at

Tyme Square. Some of the comedians looking for a new Wednesday night spot began to hit Yum Yums. I was no Tom Webb, nor was Yum Yums Tyme Square, but it was cool to be able to somewhat fill that void for the comedians on the south side of town.

APRIL 22, 2010

THE PAST MONTH was good to me. At Eddie B's last show, I got a chance to meet actress Wendy Raquel Robinson (*The Steve Harvey Show* and *The Game*) as well as comedian Gary "G. Thang" Johnson, who seemingly fell in love with my cousin Cherie that night. They were in town courtesy of the stage play they were currently starring in alongside Brian McKnight and Vivica A. Fox.

That weekend Deva and I had our own stage play business to handle. The two of us went downtown and passed out two thousand flyers for *Me, You & Your Wife: You Need to Choose*. On April 10th, we performed the stage play in Houston at the Stafford Civic Center in front of an audience of six hundred people. Deva wrote me a part in the play making it the first time I had performed in a play since high school. It felt good to grace the stage as an actor again. I played the role of a homosexual by the name of Peaches. Don't laugh.

The coolest thing April has offered so far is my first performance at Houston's premier comedy stage, The Improv. Leroy Williams hooked me up by allowing me to host one of his Hypnosis & Comedy shows. I didn't expect the opportunity to perform there would come as soon as it did. I had a good set and found performing on that stage easier than some of the bars I have performed at. The feeling was amazing!

AFTER THE APRIL 22, 2010 entry, I stopped writing. I'm not 100% sure why, but I believe it was because I lost my notebook. The thought of publishing my journal had not yet crossed my mind, so I didn't find it too important to buy another notebook and continue writing. By the time I found my lost notebook, over two years had passed. That's a lot of missing time.

Fortunately, in November of 2010, I started keeping a daily log of where I performed each night. With the help of that performance log, I will recap some key moments during this vacant time. I've underlined the following entries to help distinguish the recapped entries from the ones I wrote in real time.

Let's continue the journey!

5

And Then There Was This Girl, Right?

MAY 6, 2010

I WAS INVITED by comedian Brandy Adams to a poetry show to perform comedy a few weeks prior. It would be my first-time meeting Brandy Adams after already being Facebook friends with her for a while. I enjoyed performing at the show, and I met a few poets that night.

The most notable poet I met was Choice who informed me of a poetry night on Tuesdays at the Legendary Mr. A's night club in the Fifth Ward of Houston, TX. I don't recall having a great set that night. I do recall, however, getting into a tense exchange with one of the poets after making a joke about Fifth Ward. Thankfully, things didn't get too out of hand. Fighting isn't one of my greatest strengths.

Despite the near dust up, the host of the show, Black Snow,

(a legend in his own right) approached me afterwards and invited me to another venue where he hosted poetry.

I went to Under the Bridge that very next Thursday. It was a nice place and very close to my home. As I waited for my turn to perform, a young woman walked in late. I didn't pay her much attention, initially. Sometime later, one of the poets was up front reciting a spoken word piece about homeless people. Again, I wasn't paying much attention as I browsed the web on my phone.

When I looked up I realized it was the same young lady that had walked in late. However, this time I paid a lot of attention. She was beautiful. How could I not have noticed before? There was something about her voice and her look that had me captivated. She finished her piece and Black Snow told the audience to "Give it up for Sandrell Ross."

JUNE 10, 2010

IT WAS BOUND to happen sooner or later. They say you're not really a comedian until it happens. Well, on this night it happened. For the first time, I got booed off stage.

There was a hot new comedy room on Thursday nights at The Horn. The show was hosted by Ali Siddiq. Ali is the guy that all the young comics looked up to in Houston. For many years he was the lone guy that non-Houston comedians knew. He was also the lone guy in the city who could consistently pack out a show at the time.

When the shows at The Horn first took off, all the comedians from well-seasoned vets to bland newbies flocked to perform there. The place was packed every week. The veteran comedians had the place rocking. The newbies, not so much. For us, performing at The Horn was intimidating because the crowd would boo you if you weren't good. In fact, Ali encouraged it!

Ali was out of town when I made my debut at The Horn. Kier Spates hosted in his absence. Kier, in my opinion, was the funniest comedian in Houston. His high-pitched voice made his already funny bits even more hysterical. You may know Kier as Junior on *The Steve Harvey Morning Show*.

Okay, so I'm stalling a bit. You're probably hoping I get to the booing part already, and I shall. I was nervous about performing so I decided to have a couple beers to help my nerves. It was a foolish decision.

Kier called me to the stage and I had a nice start. I was about three minutes into my set and beginning to think I could go the distance. I was feeling good considering most of the newbies barely made it to their second joke. I made it to Joke Five.

Perhaps the audience expected me to fail all along because as soon as that fifth joke flopped, they let me have it. I couldn't recover. I picked up my tail, tucked it in my butt, and humbly walked off stage to a chorus of boos. It didn't help that among those booing were NBA all-stars Dwight Howard and Rashard Lewis.

In the aftermath, I could see why people believe that getting booed makes you a better comedian. My worst fear was now behind me. I tasted the ultimate fail onstage and survived it. Now I could be great!

NOVEMBER 17, 2010

WHEN I STARTED DOING COMEDY, I had the utmost respect for anyone who had been performing longer than me, even if it was just a day. If a comedian was on TV, that person was automatically a guru in my mind.

So when I was able to get a comedian (name omitted for privacy) I had seen on television to headline my comedy night at Yum Yums for the first time, I was stoked. He was a nine-time BET ComicView veteran originally from Houston. Now living in L.A, he traveled back to his hometown occasionally to do shows. He was funny, and he had some nice bits with a distinctive, hiccup-like laugh that he effectively used to set up his punch lines.

I had met him a year earlier at one of Eddie B's shows. He always put on a great show and my audience loved him. The struggles I had with him were over performance fees.

The first time he performed on my show for cheap. However, every time he was in town and wanted to do my room, the price would go up. Don't get me wrong; I like to pay people and in a lot of cases I overpay. The problem was that Yum Yums was a free show. I didn't charge people to enjoy comedy. I got paid by the club and it wasn't much. I often paid artist out of my own pocket. Any show where I featured a working comedian, I lost money—a habit that haunted me for a long time.

Having said that, the gentleman was a talented artist and businessman who was not wrong to ask for the money increases. I was wrong for agreeing to it though. I booked him on one more show before I eventually became firm and said, "No." It wasn't easy. I'm a nice guy and perhaps a people pleaser to a fault. Yet I had to do it for my own business to survive.

I don't write this entry to bash the comedian. He's a great guy! It is important, however, for young artists and bookers to know this lesson when they are first starting out. You don't have to work deals that make no financial sense whatsoever. Don't put yourself in the dark on purpose. It is not necessary. If you are good at what you do, opportunities will come as you work hard and perfect your craft.

NOVEMBER 24, 2010

HERE WE ARE, back at Yum Yums. This may have been the best, and my personal favorite, show that I ever hosted at the little club on Boone Rd. (It's between this one and my second MickeyLodeon Fest, which I will detail in the next chapter.)

This night had all the makings of a great show. It was the day before Thanksgiving and my dad's family was in town from Flint, MI for the holidays. It was my dad's birthday too so I had some of the comedians roast him on stage. The show had everything including a comedy contest.

The contest itself provided the only stain on an otherwise great night. Four comedians competed that night, yet only two come to mind, Demetria Dixon and Lil T. Lil T happens to be the son of H-Town rapper, Lil Troy, who had the hit song "Wanna Be a Baller" in the late '90s.

Anyway, those comedians come to mind because Demetria Dixon won, but I would find out later that it should've been Lil T.

Kena, who was one of the judges told me after the show that I called the wrong winner. It was an honest mistake. I was handed a piece of paper with names of the comedians on it. Demetria's name was circled so I figured that's who the judges were going with.

I figured wrong because on the flipside of that paper was Lil T's name written alone. This would not be the last time I would make a gaff when announcing a winner. I guess you could say I was Steve Harvey before Steve Harvey.

I felt bad for the mistake especially for Lil T because he missed out on the prize money. Ultimately, it was an awesome night, even with a flawed contest.

DECEMBER 5, 2010

I WAS ONCE FEATURED in a magazine—S.I.A. (Supporting Independent Artists). In addition to me and a few other comedians, the magazine featured musicians, actors, and poets. One of those poets happened to be the girl I had a huge crush on, Sandrell Ross.

On this night, the 5th, the founders of the magazine held a release party showcasing some of the artists featured in the first issue, myself included. Punkin from Pluto, a talented singer and poet, served as the headliner of the event, and rightfully so considering she graced the front cover.

Earlier that day, I attended the Houston Auto Show for the first time. It's the biggest auto show the city hosts, and I absolutely had to go. Not because I love cars, however, that's more my dad's passion. Instead, my buddy Ken Boyd was hosting the "Next to Blow" stage. This was a big deal. While it wasn't the main stage that featured artists such as Chris Brown and others, it did serve as great exposure for Ken.

DECEMBER 24, 2010

I WALKED outside and to my pleasant surprise Sandrell was waiting for me. This had to be the moment where I was like "Yooo, this girl is going to be my girlfriend." It confirmed the same thought I had a day or two before when she came to see me, making it the first time I ever had a visitor while I was in jail.

That's right, due to my inability to obey traffic laws and my refusal, or more accurately my fear of going to court, I landed in the Harris County jail. On the night of the arrest, I was leaving Eddie B's show at Carrington's and I mistakenly took Buffalo Speedway through the hot, residential, West University subdivision.

I spent a long, gruesome three nights in jail. I never thought while in jail that I would have to spend a phone call on a comedian, but that's exactly what happened. The call was made to my good friend Adam Bob. The request was simple, "Hey man, can you host Yum Yums for me?" to which he replied in the most Adam Bobest way possible, "Already Man!"

The call to A. Beezy really served me well because we were scheduled to be on a show together the upcoming Thursday at Club Ovations, which was ironically located in the same West University neighborhood I was arrested in. Maybe it was good that I couldn't make it. In any case, Adam Bob was able to notify the powers that be of my absence. (You may be thinking, "This guy spent more time in jail than onstage." Well, you'd be wrong. I only went eight times.)

Getting back to my release, Sandrell picked me up from jail, and while I don't remember how the day was spent, I vividly remember the night.

We accompanied each other to the Improv where Ali was holding his annual Gift of Laughter Christmas Comedy Show. The show featured Houston's top comedians and was really dope. Afterwards, I walked Sandrell to her car, not because I'm just nice like that, but because she was taking me home. Once inside, we got into a playful wrestling match for possession of one of our cell phones.

One thing led to another and the next thing you know, magic was happening.

On second thought, perhaps that is when I knew she'd be my girl.

AHH! What's a story without a little romance? It was fun having a girlfriend. I didn't have many growing up. Two to be exact and both while I was in fifth grade. (What a year that was!)
I didn't have many birthday parties either, but that changed when I became an adult. Let me tell you about the best one ever.

6

MickeyLodeon Fest 2

JANUARY 5, 2011

AFTER RUNNING "It Iz What It Iz Wednezdayz" at Yum Yums for nine months, I decided I would start charging patrons to attend the show. I did this for two reasons. One was obviously to make a little extra cash. Secondly, I wanted to train the audience to respect the show a little more.

Yum Yums was usually a tough room to play. There were some great shows at times where the turnout was awesome and everyone listened and enjoyed themselves. Then there were dreadful nights where people spent their time drinking by the bar and talking endlessly throughout the show.

On this night, I decided to celebrate the last free night of comedy at Yum Yums. I promoted it well and I had comedians Adam Bob, Donnie Johnson, and Terry Gross come tear the house down.

The night was great, and it gave me confidence that the cover charge would work. I charged $5 at the door for the next three weeks. Unfortunately, my crowds began to thin so I canned the experiment and comedy night was free again. The club had too many regulars there accustomed to free entry and some scoffed at having to pay.

But hey, at least I tried.

Sometimes my old karaoke buddy Charles would come perform at my comedy night. He still wasn't any good, but when I told him that his first performance served as one of my biggest inspirations to do comedy, he was floored. I don't think my words have ever made someone as happy as they made Charles at that moment. He would go on to tell everyone:
"You know, I'm the reason Mickey started comedy."

FEBRUARY 11, 2011

MY LOVE for karaoke was no secret. Perhaps that's why Netra Babin asked me to host her Comedy and Karaoke night in her absence. Her show was held at Scott Gertner's Sports Bar. Scott Gertner's, now under new ownership and known as Prospect Park, was one of the most popular sports bars in Houston. I was super stoked to be the host for a night, but not just because I was playing a cool venue and singing songs. I was extra geeked out because it marked the first time that I would see my name in lights.

The marquee out front read:

"Friday – Comedy & Karaoke hosted by Mickey Housley."

Amazing!

FEBRUARY 15, 2011

THERE WAS an upstart promoter by the name of Jason Smith who was trying his hand at producing comedy shows. He started TakeOva Tuesdays on the Northside in Greenspoint at a venue known as Stilettos. Jason pegged Ken Boyd as the host and Ken quickly recruited Adam Bob and me to do the first show. Eddie B was also booked as the headliner.

This show stands out to me because it was kind of my coming out party. I had a really great set and it sort of kick-started a pretty good year for me on stage. Also, I believe it was the first time Sandrell's family saw me perform.

I remember the buildup being pretty good for this show as well. A few days before the show, Jason set up a night for the comedians to promote TakeOva Tuesdays on an internet radio show.

I was rather quiet on air and deferred a bit as Ken, Adam, and Eddie all had their shining moments. The hosts of the radio show attended Stilettos and I remember them telling me that they were shocked at how funny I was after being so dry during the interview. That was cool for me to hear because I always preferred giving the audience an element of surprise.

The show was extremely successful overall. Jason didn't take over many Tuesdays after that, but with his help and through the developing bond of Ken, Adam Bob, and me, we would go on to produce several more shows together.

MARCH 9, 2011

IT WAS the Second Annual MickeyLodeon Fest. The show was littered with dozens of comedians and poets. One of them being my good friend Rain the Poet. I was happy that she and so many artists came to support me. They all crushed it on stage as well.

This one was held at Yum Yums just as the first, and the place was jam-packed. I remember comedian Dave Lawson joking on stage, "Damn, if this is how Mickey is celebrating two years of comedy, what's he gonna have at the ten-year party? Strippers and lions?" (The ten-year party is less than two years away. I better get comfortable around strippers.)

At the end of the show the comedians roasted me and didn't stop there. They proceeded to rip the whole room. This was one of the early shows where Blame would use his "cap gun" method. He would roast someone in the audience then immediately point the gun at his target while the DJ would simultaneously play the sound effect of a loud gun shot. It's a creative and effective tactic that makes the digs more hysterical.

The night was ridiculously amazing. If I had to compare the first year to the second of MickeyLodeon, number 2 won by a landslide. This show was great because it was much more than just a show. It was a party!

I was approaching a year of hosting comedy at Yum Yums, which was cool considering my six-week flameout at Legends. In addition to the birthday shows, I had some great moments there. Unfortunately, my run at the club wouldn't survive 2011. Even more unfortunate, tragedy was involved.

7

So Long Yum Yums

MARCH 18, 2011

ON THE TWO-YEAR anniversary of the first time I ever performed standup, I was privileged to do a cool show with Comedian Marcus D. Wiley of the *Yolanda Adams Morning Show*. The setting was Beaumont, TX at the Jefferson Theatre. It was for some sort of convention that involved representatives of the NAACP as well as top executives of the H.E.B. grocery store chain.

Marcus Wiley asked his good friend Blame to recruit some young comedians to open for him at the show. Blame grabbed Ken Boyd, Adam Bob, Stacy Anderson, and me. Sandrell also came along and kicked off the show with a nice poetry selection. The show went great and afterwards two of the H.E.B. executives treated us all to dinner at Red Lobster.

One of the gentlemen told us to order whatever we wanted. We did just that, and he didn't seem to mind too much when the bill came around. That is until he noticed that one of us ordered something a tad more expensive than everyone else.

"WHO ORDERED THE LOBSTER?" he shouted!

I was so embarrassed.

It was Sandrell.

MAY 13, 2011

BY NOW IT'S probably no secret that I had formed a tight bond with Ken and Adam Bob. (I don't think I've ever called Adam by his first name alone. It's always been either Adam Bob or A. Beezy.) We had all done several shows together and often spent late nights joking around after shows or soaking up wisdom from the vets. In fact, Ken was the other recipient of those Eddie Griffin chest punches I mentioned earlier.

One night we were hanging out at The Horn when Billy Sorrells approached us about doing our own official show —a show for our class. The three of us along with a few others that all started in 2008. The other comedian with us that night was Darwin Prater, better known as Sticks or the friend that woke me up in Killeen, Tx. Sticks was a good friend of ours, but he didn't take comedy as serious as the rest of us. It was more or less an idea he was flirting with until his unemployment ran out.

Billy never put the show together, but Ken, Adam Bob, and I decided we would proceed with the idea and produce a show featuring ourselves exclusively. As a trio, we formed a dynamic group with each man having his own distinct style and personality.

Ken was confident and brash. Very charismatic. There was no telling what would come out of his mouth. They called him "Ken 2 the Fool" for a reason. I'm careful not to call him wild as he didn't smoke or drink. He had some sense if not a lot.

Adam Bob started performing in his early thirties, so he was like the uncle of the group so to speak. He was a nice guy and fun with high energy. We would kid him about how loud he was on stage sometimes. He had a happy-go-lucky kind of demeanor. I saw him get mad maybe once ever.

I was silly, yet just as often subdued—always good for a witty remark or well-timed zinger. According to them, I was the one with the morals.

We were all funny, talented, young, and up and coming comedians. We had a solid product in place. We even came up with a dope name, The Maks of Comedy. It's an acronym made from our names: Mickey, Adam, and Ken. Sticks could've been the "S."

Jason Smith served as our manager and helped us with the business details. Oh yes, we were for real about this thing.

On May 13th we had our first show at the Avani Lounge. The turnout was decent, if not great.

Sandrell opened our show with some poetry. (She was with me a lot.) I can't remember who hosted and featured between my two amigos. We mutually agreed that I would close the show, as I was perhaps the strongest performer at the time. I think Ken deserves that distinction now.

We did a few more shows before eventually fading away. We all live in different cities now and don't communicate as much, but when the three of us get together, it's always a good time.

Please believe we are still the Maks!

JUNE 6, 2011

LEROY WILLIAMS, a man who has awarded me many cool experiences, offered yet another when he asked me to help write for a pilot that a producer friend of his was developing. He asked me to invite a few others to help with the project. Of course, I hit up Ken, Adam Bob, and Sandrell.

We all met with Leroy at Uptown Tappas where comedian Lil Brough ran an open mic on Mondays. Leroy introduced us to his producer friend John Wayne, founder of Londyn Town Productions. He shared with us his vision of producing a comedy sitcom titled *The Breakroom*. He also mentioned that we would receive a writer's credit for our contributions to the show—a totally sweet deal.

We would convene at Leroy's house once a week to brainstorm and learn some nuances of writing and producing a sitcom. We had fun, and this proved to be an important experience for me. It showed me that creating a television series or movie is possible. It's not just some cool thing we see on TV that you and I—the common folk—are incapable of producing. We may not be Spike. We may not be Tarantino. But we can do it, man!

JUNE 23, 2011

FOR TWENTY PLUS years the city of Houston would determine the funniest comedian by holding the Houston's Funniest Person contest. I sucked the first time I did it. The next year, for whatever reason, I wasn't aware it even took place. In 2011, however, I *was* aware and made sure I signed up.

There were several preliminary rounds in the weeks leading up to the finals. I competed in the first preliminary and was one of two comedians, along with Gerald Torregosa, selected to advance to the finals. Adam Bob advanced the following week and I remember the two of us putting a little pressure on Ken who was doing his preliminary round the week after A. Beezy.

"Hey two-thirds of the Maks made it to the finals. It's on you man," we joked.

46

By the time the big night came around three-thirds of the Maks made it to the finals. It was held at the Laff Spot, not to be confused with the Laff Stop, which had closed two years before. When I got there, I was surprised, and a bit flattered to learn that I was one of the favorites to win.

I believed I was funny, and I put in some work. I can say with confidence that I was onstage more than any other comedian in Houston during 2010 and early 2011. However, I didn't imagine that I was a favorite. Heck, I was halfway surprised when I advanced to the finals. It felt like a quick ascension after getting bounced out of the competition so quickly the last time I did it.

I was a little nervous as I usually am when doing a contest, but for the most part I felt good. I had been practicing well and even fasted in preparation for the contest. Having family and friends in attendance sure helped too.

Out of twelve finalists, I drew number 7, which is a sweet spot. I went up and delivered a great set. I remember the owner, Don Learned, coming out to the lobby immediately after my set and going, "Yo, this kid just knocked it out of the park."

It was his first time seeing me. And he wasn't the only comedy club booker that took notice. Raymond Cook was a judge that night. From what I was told, he was quite impressed. I had never heard of nor met the general manager of the Houston Improv before this night, but I'm glad he liked me.

I felt good for a moment about my chances of winning. That feeling faded when Theodore M.E. Taylor took the stage. He began to rock the crowd. Theo was doing so well that I couldn't watch anymore. I literally walked out of the comedy club.

After the performances, the comedians gathered inside as we eagerly awaited the results. "In 3rd place, Gerald Torregosa. In Second place... Mickey Housley."

Theo won, and deservingly so. I heard some whispers that I should've won, but honestly, I disagree. Theo had a great set, and the victory may have been a bit of revenge for him. Theo was the one forced to settle for second place in the 4th of July contest that I won when I first started performing standup.

Second place initially sucks when you're so close, but after the sting of defeat subsided a bit, I realize it was nothing to hang my head at. In fact, it's one of my prouder moments in standup, and I still use it as a credit six years later. If you enter Mickey Housley in Wikipedia nothing will come up. But if you type in Houston's Funniest Person Contest and scroll down to winners and runners-up, you'll see me floating around there somewhere.

As a consolation prize, Don expressed interest in booking me at the Laff Spot, but that never happened.

The club closed the very next week.

The closing of the Laff Spot left the fourth largest city in the U.S. with just two comedy clubs. There were four when I started and as many as nine in the late '80s.

AUGUST 10, 2011

SOMETIME IN EARLY AUGUST, Steve, the owner of Yum Yums, suffered a brain aneurysm while attending a concert leaving him severely injured. Brain aneurysms give me the chills. When I was a teenager, a woman I went to church with passed away suddenly after suffering from one. They have a mortality rate of 40% and can happen without warning.

Almost immediately I put together a "Get Well Uncle Steve" show at Yum Yums. I held it on my usual comedy night and many people came for his sake. I bought a card and had all his friends and regulars at the bar sign it. Several comedians came to support as well—one of them being Leroy.

Leroy brought a guest with him too—a comedian by the name of Shucky Ducky. You may remember Mr. Ducky from Def Comedy Jam with his signature phrase "Shucky ducky, quack quack." He was now the ringmaster of the national touring UniverSoul Circus, which is why he was in town.

It would have been cool to have Shucky grace my stage, but he declined to perform when I asked. No matter, because he did something even cooler four days later.

It was Sandrell's birthday, and I decided I'd do something real special. I took her to the circus. It feels kind of lame as I write this, but hey, Leroy gave us free tickets.

At some point during the show, Shucky was walking through the stands engaging the crowd. He then walked right by us and we grabbed his attention. After taking a quick moment to recognize us, he says, "Oh hey, what's up? Y'all came!"

He asked us to remind him of our names. After doing so he disappeared, and later reemerged in the center of the big top tent.

"Hey everybody. There are two very talented comedians in the house tonight." (Sandrell had recently converted from poet to comedian.)

"As I ask them to stand, would you please give a big round of applause for Mickey and Cherelle." (No one ever gets Sandrell's name right.)

And what a resounding applause we received. It was such a cool moment. We felt so honored. People were coming up to us afterwards asking when our next show was. It's good to have cards for random moments like those.

That week Sandrell and I went to see Steve in the hospital. Unfortunately, they weren't allowing visitors at the time, but we were at least able to leave the card we signed for him at Yum Yums.

Although we're Facebook friends, I haven't seen or spoken to Steve since he suffered the aneurysm. His sister, Belinda eventually took over the club. Through her, I learned that he moved to Dallas and was being taken care of by their mother. I pray he's okay and hope to see him again one day.

SEPTEMBER 5, 2011

BILLY HOUSLEY JR. (my dad) is quite the character. He is a great guy, kind-hearted, and fun to be around. Yet those who know him best will point to his fixation on women and money as his greatness weaknesses.

He was always looking for more ways to score cash. His methods ranged from working two jobs to religiously playing the lotto. And then there's his never-dying quest to strike it big in the network marketing world. He had been a fan ever since a coworker introduced him to Prepaid Legal (now Legal Shield) back in 2007.

Fascinated by the concept and more importantly the compensation that Prepaid Legal offered, Billy quickly invited his sons to check out the business at one of the weekly meetings. Being one of those sons I was also intrigued by this foreign (to me at the time) business format.

I didn't achieve much with Prepaid Legal nor the other two or three network marketing businesses that I tried over the next couple of years, but I do believe they are a viable way to make a living with the right work ethic and mindset.

My greatest moment in network marketing would come a few short years later with a company I never even signed up for. Somewhere around late 2010, a new brand popped up that suddenly became all the rage in network marketing.

Organo Gold made their bones selling coffee and all the entrepreneurs were flocking to them, including Emanuel Bernstein who was one of the Prepaid Legal superstars. In September, they held a huge national convention that spanned three days. There was a conference exclusively for the men on Friday and one exclusively for the women on Saturday.

The women hired a hypnotist to provide entertainment for their event. But it wasn't just any old hypnotist, they hired the Hypnobro. Leroy asked Sandrell and I to attend the conference to help him with his show. Helping Leroy mainly consisted of pulling chairs off stage when people were unable to be hypnotized. Sometimes women, while in a trance, exposed themselves and I had to cover them with a towel or jacket.

Leroy kind of surprised me when he asked if I wanted to perform a few minutes up top. Of course, I did. I took the stage and performed in front of fourteen hundred women. It was my largest audience up to that point. Rocking a crowd of that magnitude has a different kind of sizzle. The laughs have a way of booming at you so hard you can feel it. It was an incredible experience, and with so many women there, I know one thing for sure, Pops would've loved it.

My dad was seeing a woman on the side name Patricia. Everyone called her Trish for short, but I was respectful. I called her Miss Triss!

SEPTEMBER 29, 2011

THE WEEKLY WRITING sessions at Leroy's house were going fine. We had added Netra Babin to the fold to give the show another female perspective. At one of the sessions, Leroy presented us with an enticing treat.

He had an upcoming weekend booked at the Comedy Showcase and decided he would use one of the days to allow his young team of writers a chance to showcase at the club. This was a big deal to us as none of us had been booked at the Showcase before. We were thrilled!

Netra, Ken, and I met at Adam Bob's crib to help each other fine-tune jokes that we were working on. Sandrell spent time working with Leroy and veteran comedian Frank Overton. There was concern that Sandrell wouldn't do well as she had only recently started doing comedy. We all wanted the show to be very good.

While out for lunch one day, Ken and I had a friendly debate over who would sell the most tickets for the show. After some banter, I figured I'd raise the ante.

"Okay how about this," I started, "If you sell more tickets than me, I'll let you have the headlining duties."

Ken's eyes got huge. Leroy initially pegged me to headline the show and my competitive fire pushed me to put it on the line. It was a costly mistake.

Neither of us were really known for bringing a bunch of

people to our shows, but the bet lit a fire into Ken. A beast had awakened. Ken would easily outsell me by a count of 165 to 11. It wasn't a fluke either. Ken would eventually do shows at the Improv and would sell north of 250 tickets.

With the day of the show nearing and the venue just about sold out, it was time to settle the payment arrangement. John Wayne presented each of us with a contract to look over and sign. That's when things took a turn for the worse.

Although Sandrell and I didn't oppose much, the crew didn't agree with how the money was being distributed. The frustration was understandable, especially in Ken's case considering he was the most responsible for the show being sold out. Our disdain at the contract outraged Leroy. His defense was that he didn't have to put us on his show, which I felt was true. I was caught in the middle between my friends and my mentor.

Ultimately, a settlement was made. We all received a small bump in pay with Ken appropriately receiving a tad bit more. We continued with the show, and it turned out to be amazing.

As expected, the place was packed. Leroy hosted and brought up Sandrell first, who to our delight did quite well. I was happy for her. It was her first real show as a comedian, and nobody gave her a chance. After Sandrell's performance we knew we were in for a special night. Adam Bob went next and absolutely destroyed it. The writing sessions and extra open mics were paying big dividends.

Netra went after Adam Bob and murdered it. I followed her with one of my best sets. Ken got a stirring ovation the moment he was introduced to the stage and he did not disappoint. The show was phenomenal from start to finish. However, it didn't fully diffuse the bad blood that had brewed over the contract dispute.

Leroy mutually parted ways with everyone from the writing project save Sandrell and me. The two of us would continue to work with Leroy over the years. Adam Bob remained cordial with him as well as Ken to a lesser extent, but Netra couldn't stand him. In fact, she cussed him out after the show before storming out.

Despite the madness that ensued, I still look back on this show very fondly. I think we all do.

OCTOBER 11, 2011

I PREVIOUSLY MENTIONED that comedian Lil Brough ran an open mic at Uptown Tappas on Monday nights. There were actually two open mics ran at the hookah bar during the week. Rich Williams hosted comedy there on Tuesdays.

On one of those Tuesday nights there was a female comedian on the verge of stardom visiting from Los Angeles by the name of Tiffany Haddish. Yes, that Tiffany Haddish— the one from *Girls Trip* and *The Carmichaels*. She was not well-known outside of the comedy realm at the time.

After working out some new material, she and a good friend of hers were looking for a place to kick it. Somehow karaoke came up, and since I knew several spots, they asked me to lead the way. They followed me to a joint about five minutes away called the Zanzi Bar. The three of us sang songs all night and hung out until about three in the morning. It was a great time.

Fast forward one year, I saw Tiffany in L.A. at the Comedy Union. Ecstatic, I said,

"Hey Tiffany, it's me Mickey. Remember when I hung out with you? —and your best friend—in Houston—a little over a year ago—we did karaoke and all."

She didn't have a single clue. She wasn't rude about it at all, she just didn't remember.

It sucked a little bit, I'm not going to lie, but it's cool because Tiffany taught me something during that first encounter in Houston. While hanging with her she said multiple times "I'm gonna be a star!" and "I'm gonna be famous!"

After seeing me do standup and karaoke she kindly made the same declarations about my career as well. I hear people often talk about the power of words and speaking things into existence, but with Tiffany I saw it first-hand.

Now she's in commercials, sitcoms, and movies. It's awesome to witness her shine and launch towards the top of the game.

She said we were going to be stars, and so far, she's halfway right.

OCTOBER 19, 2011

HOSTING Yum Yums every Wednesday often meant I couldn't hang at other shows around the city, namely The Horn, which Ali had moved from Thursday nights to Wednesday.

On this night, however, I thought to myself, "What the heck. *I'm gonna skip out on Yum Yums and go to The Horn.*" It sounds bad as is, but it gets worse. This was the fourth consecutive time I skipped hosting my show. I had started to dread doing the show. The crowds had become paper thin, and Steve was no longer steering the ship. I had tried getting out of doing the show before, but Steve always fought against the idea.

I wouldn't say I used Steve's health issues as a way out, but I do realize that it's difficult to suggest otherwise. It wasn't even a full two months since Steve suffered his brain aneurysm before I bolted. Trust me, I wasn't proud of myself for just fading away without at least discussing matters with his sister. At least I can take comfort in knowing that I wouldn't have been there much longer anyway as Yum Yums shut down a few months later.

Thinking back, I'm glad Steve pushed me to do the show. Hosting comedy there for nearly two years played a big factor in my growth as a comedian. There were times of beauty and there were times of struggle, but looking back I can appreciate them both.

With the demise of Yum Yums, a chapter in my young career had ended. However, a new one would soon begin as I started to travel a bit.

8

California Love

NOVEMBER 16, 2011

SPEAKING OF THE HORN, I was once part of an epic showdown there. Ali and Terry Gross got into a bout of bravado claiming that one could put a funnier team of comedians together than the other.

On November 9th the two funnymen held a comedy draft. I wasn't at The Horn the night of the draft, but I was informed that I was selected by Team Gross. The following Wednesday it was go time.

Here's how the teams broke down:

Team Ali	Team Gross
Eddie B	Mickey Housley
Stacy Anderson	Jenifer Jourmany
Joe P (Poet)	Khalid (Poet)
John Gard	Derrick Keener
Billy Sorrells	Blame

I went first and didn't have a great set, but the old dance bit I used to do imitating Destiny's Child saved me. I was very distracted that night as Sandrell and I were having a rough patch in our relationship and had temporarily broken up.

The rest of the show went great. Eddie B and Billy were particularly good for Team Ali, and Joe P moved the crowd with a fierce spoken word piece. Jennifer, Derrick, and Blame did the heavy lifting for Team Gross.

Throughout the performances Terry and Ali served as the co-host of the competition and they were extremely competitive. They were arguably the two funniest comedians in the city. They used to co-host Houston's famed Just Joking Comedy Club in the late '90s. From then on, they would always have this on, off, on-again, off-again relationship. This night it appeared to be the off-again version.

Going by DJ GT's (arguably Houston's top DJ and Ali's best friend) unofficial score card, Team Gross was the winner with a count of 3–2. However, a crowd vote determined the winner to be Team Ali. They won and split the prize money that was north of $3,500. Well, they split the majority of the bread. Ali generously gave a portion of the winnings to the defeated team.

If you ask me, everybody won. In my opinion, it was one of the dopest moments in Houston Comedy.

I never did the Destiny's Child routine after this show. The routine got me standing ovations and won me a contest. The audience loved it, but the comedians hated it and several of the older comics discouraged me from doing it. Their reasoning was that I couldn't do such a gag on TV. While this is true and I'm sure I wouldn't be doing the routine at this point anyway, I regret that I trashed it prematurely.

My advice: Do what works for you. It's good to get insight from more experienced comics, but carefully consider if the criticism is helpful and not hateful. The only time a comedian should tell you not to do a joke is if you're stealing it. Aside from that, let no one constrict your funny.

NOVEMBER 22, 2011

THE LONGEST I had ever driven on the road was nine hours from Houston to Tunica, MS. Sandrell and Leroy were with me, but I drove the entire way there and on a suspended license at that.

Leroy was booked at a Funny Bone Comedy Club inside of Harrah's Casino. It was my first time performing inside a casino. Right across from Funny Bone was Paula Dean's restaurant. I wasn't too familiar with Ms. Dean at the time and didn't bother to dine at her establishment. This was before she got in trouble for having a case of loose lips.

We had a long run of nine shows in six days that all fared nicely. The lengthy stay allowed us to do some sightseeing in Memphis, TN, which is just a half hour north of Tunica.

Trotting through Beale St. for the first time was indeed a treat. There's a lot of culture in Memphis with it being a hotbed for blues music and the home of many great musicians such as Elvis Presley and Isaac Hayes. Both of those greats have a blue note engraved on the street with their name on it reminiscent of the stars in Hollywood.

One of those blue notes that we noticed belonged to a man by the name of Clyde Hopkins. It read, "The Godfather of Blues." As we looked up, the ninety-year-old legend was standing right beside us promoting his new album outside of a record store. It was amazing to see a man at such a ripe age still performing and hustling. Perhaps that'll be me 60 years from now telling jokes. After all, Dick Gregory and Don Rickles did it.

The flipside to our trip was spending Thanksgiving away from our families. Sandrell had relatives in Memphis, but they were having dinner late, which conflicted with the show we had to do later that evening. We ended up eating Thanksgiving dinner at a Piccadilly's.

It wasn't the worst, but Paula Dean's would've been better.

MARCH 9, 2012

THE FIRST TWO MickeyLodeon Fests were held at Yum Yums and had success, particularly the second one. With Yum Yums no longer in play, I made a change in venue and chose to hold my show at the Palm Palace, a banquet hall located in the Greenspoint neighborhood in northwest Houston.

I didn't have a huge turnout at MickeyLodeon 3—fifty people maybe. And besides myself I only had three performers: Ken, Adam Bob, and Blame. A far cry from the dozens I had at MickeyLodeon 2. Although this one didn't have the epic feel of the year before, it did advance the series. It kept MickeyLodeon going, and moving it from a bar to a banquet hall was an important step.

MAY 16, 2012

PERIODICALLY, there were comedy shows held at Walker's Barbecue in downtown Houston. On this night I remember comedian Tony Rock, younger brother of Chris Rock, accompanying his cousin Bobby Roberts to the show. Bobby, a New York native, had been living and doing comedy in Houston for several years.

This was the second time I met Tony. However, it was the first time I really got to speak and connect with him. It was Ken though who made a lasting impression. Ken challenged him to a game of pool and the two began to bond as the night went on.

On the way out, I mentioned to Tony that I would be in L.A. real soon. He said "cool" and told me to take his number, which I thought was super dope!

Young comedians get pumped over that type of stuff.

MAY 18, 2012

AFTER A FEW YEARS OF PERFORMING, comedians gain the confidence to travel to Oakland to compete in the infamous Bay Area Competition. The contest is legendary. Some of its past participants include Mike Epps, Jamie Foxx and Katt Williams.

I too was once one of those young hopefuls. Boarding a plane for the first time, and nervous as heck, I took flight to Northern California. Sandrell got a kick out of this and recorded my timid face on her phone. How I got the money to even make the trip was a blessing from God.

Walking my neighborhood, as I do every morning, I came across a man hosting a garage sale. I had never bought anything from a garage sale before or even cared to for that matter, but this one had something unique up for grabs. A motorcycle.

It was a 1981 Honda Goldwing. For reference, Prince rode

a Goldwing in his "Purple Rain" video. This wasn't Prince's bike, however. There were issues with its transmission, so the man was only asking $100 for it. I mulled it over for a moment and decided to purchase. It sat in my apartment for months until I needed cash for the trip to Oakland. I created an ad on Craigslist and $400 later I was off to the Bay.

The weekend was great. I got to meet a lot of comedians. Some were new up-and-comers and some were established professionals such as Laura Hayes and Don "DC" Curry. There were helpful workshops and discussion panels throughout the event. As for the contest portion, it was bittersweet.

As great as the Bay Area Contest was, it was quite often accused of being rigged and showing favoritism to certain comedians. To be fair, all contests catch a bad rap for this. Comedy is subjective and how can you *really* judge who's funnier than someone else. Dave Chappelle is the funniest comedian to me, but it could be George Lopez to the next man.

That being said, it sure felt like I got the short end of the stick when I performed that Friday night. There were four preliminary rounds. Four comedians from each round would advance to the semifinals. I had a very good set. I felt I was in the top three for sure. Apparently, the judges thought otherwise.

"Well, maybe I wasn't as good as I thought I was," I quietly thought to myself. Perhaps that was true, but then again there were several folks that approached me and said,

"Dude, you were robbed!"

Yeah, that's what I thought too, but you know what? I had a good time anyway.

P.S. Willie Lynch Jr. out of St. Louis won.

MAY 28, 2012

AFTER THE BAY AREA CONTEST, Sandrell and I caught a ride with Houston comedians Chris Owar and Canice Nnana down to Los Angeles.

My rationale for going to L.A. immediately after the Bay Area contest was simple. In three years of doing standup I had yet to make it to L.A. I didn't want to take for granted that such a trip would just happen one day just because I was a comedian.

We arrived in L.A. and shortly after we met James Brown. No, not the "Sex Machine" James Brown. The JB I'm referring to is a man we met through Leroy. As you walk through life, there are some guys you realize you may never be able to repay. JB is one of those guys to me. He graciously allowed two strangers to stay with him on Leroy's behalf. It's the type of kindness that goes underreported—the type of kindness you strive to pay forward if you can't fully pay it back.

Our stay in L.A. lasted close to a week and was uneventful. We did do a few shows, and I was able to make my way over to the Laugh Factory catching the popular Chocolate

Sundays show. There was this one guy in the audience that was laughing hysterically at every joke. I couldn't help but notice him. It was Clifton Powell. Or as I better knew him,

Pinky from *Next Friday*.

MAY 31, 2012

I'M BACK in Houston and it's now time for yet another comedy competition. This time it's the Houston's Funniest Person contest again. After finishing as the runner up last year, I was one of the favorites along with comedian Slade Ham to win.

The preliminary rounds were held at the Comedy Showcase, and I lived up to the billing in the early going. Comedian and engineer Joe Bates was doing some weird number crunching using the scores that were revealed from the judges and then posting his research on Twitter. According to his statistics (Comedy and stats, who would've thought!), I had the highest grade of every comedian in the first round.

One of the judges was Houston Latin rapper Chingo Bling. I don't know if that contest inspired him or not, but Chingo began doing standup shortly after. His large online presence enabled him to sell out clubs across the nation rather quickly.

Chingo told me I did a great job after the show. I was off to a nice start, and off to the next round.

JUNE 20, 2012

THE SEMIFINALS DIDN'T GO AS SMOOTHLY for me, but I still managed to make the finals. I failed to live up to the pre-contest hype, however, and would not be donned the funniest person in Houston. That distinction would go to Matt Broussard.

The contest was very different from years past. For starters, the finals were composed of three rounds instead of one, and each round was held at a different venue. Secondly, the winners were determined by an average score of the three final performances. In short, I knew coming into the last day of finals that I could finish no better than 3rd place. In fact, there were only two comedians that had a chance to win on the last day. That being Broussard, of course, and Barrett Goldsmith.

Coincidently, this would be the last Houston's Funniest Person Contest after a twenty-two-year run.

After winning, Matt announced to the audience that it was his one-year anniversary as a standup comedian. Local competitions rarely make or break an artist, but amazingly, Matt's confidence and career soared after this. He eventually moved to L.A. and appeared on numerous television shows, most notably Conan, as well as a half-hour special on Comedy Central.

OCTOBER 18, 2012

I WAS BACK IN BEAUMONT, TX for a comedy show. This time with Adam Bob and Terry Gross. The show was at the Orleans Pavilion, a nice venue in which I had performed before. I had opened for Huggy Lowdown of the *Tom Joyner Morning Show*.

The thing that made this show significant for me was that it was the first show I ever did radio promotion for. I'm talking about live radio, not the internet stuff. (No offense to the internet radio moguls.)

The promoter took the three of us to the station a few hours before the show and let us have some fun on the air. The experience was wonderful!

For me anyways!

ACCORDING TO MY NEXT ENTRY, I found my notebook and became eager to get back to writing. I began by detailing some moments that stuck out to me, most of which I just covered. I also made a promise to write an entry every day moving forward. I must say that I didn't come close to doing that.

9

Let's Try This Again

DECEMBER 13, 2012

WELL IT'S BEEN a little over two and a half years since I last wrote an entry in this very notebook. How it turned up blows my mind considering I thought I had lost it.

My last entry, which was in April of 2010, is incomplete. I had gone a month without writing and my hand simply ran out of gas from trying to recap everything. This time it's been a thirty-two-month hiatus. But hey, I'm rededicated. I've been a standup comedian for nearly four years now. Let's see if we can do a quick recap of the last two.

Had I finished my entry on April 22nd of 2010, I would have mentioned that I started performing on the Houston poetry scene. A legendary Houston based poet by the name of Black Snow was the man who most embraced me. He hosted many poetry spots throughout the city and presented me as the token comedian at each of them. He was the first person to have me as a feature or headliner for a show.

The poetry scene played a big factor in my growth as a performer. It's also where I met my girlfriend, Sandrell Ross. She was a poet at the time and now wears many hats including comedienne.

Later in the year, I was able to do several colleges in Texas such as Texas Southern University and Stephen F. Austin. The latter was a homecoming show where a then little-known rapper by the name of Big Sean was the headlining act.

As 2011 rolled in, I started to become a fixture on local shows. Shawn Harris stayed true to his word and put me on several of his events. Additionally, I placed 2nd in the Houston's Funniest Person Competition. My performance in the competition caught the attention of the Houston Improv general manager Raymond Cook. Soon after, I was in a regular rotation at Houston's premiere comedy club.

I got to perform with some all-time great comedians such as Paul Mooney and Pablo Francisco. Just this past weekend I opened six shows at the Houston Improv for Tommy Davidson. The feature comedian for the weekend was Paul Varghese out of Dallas, TX. He has been very helpful and insightful.

When I started doing comedy in 2009, I always said 2012 would be my year. It has arguably been my most disappointing. I didn't work nearly as hard as I should have, and the year has flown past. However, it's had a few great moments. I went to California for the first time and competed in the Bay Area Comedy Competition. I also got to perform at J. Anthony Brown's comedy club, the J. Spot, in L.A.

I can't say I am completely caught up because of course I missed a lot, but at least we have a better idea of what's been going on these past couple of years. I plan to write an entry every day save Sundays and sometimes Saturday.

If this journal gets published, which is my goal, I want to thank God for bringing me back to writing. I suppose at some point, perhaps today, a certain truth finally made sense to me—I need to be proactive every day of my life. I do not need to waste time fearing if a project will fail, or make sense, or even get finished.

Pray for me.

Adios, and thanks for being patient these last two years.

Shawn Harris once paid me $100 for a show in all ones. He told me to count it, but I told him there was no need. "I trust you big homie," I said.

I got home and realized I should've counted the money. It only added up to $99. You owe me a dollar, Shawn!

DECEMBER 25, 2012

MERRY CHRISTMAS TO ALL. Hope your day was blessed.

It was for me. This week has been cool when I think about it. If I had to give a quick rundown, it would go like this:

A play and family show with Deva Mack, a highly entertaining comedy show with Blame, and a daytime gig at a restaurant. And, oh yeah, the Mayans were wrong!

Well, that's about it. Not much to elaborate on for now. However, I am currently reading "Last Words" by the legendary comedian George Carlin, and it's just starting to get good. I'm a big fan of the early years of entertainers. That probably better explains why I'm writing this journal.

Anyways, more on both books later.

JANUARY 2, 2013

HAPPY NEW YEAR, folks. I'm fairly happy. I look at 2013 as an opportunity to advance in my career—advancing in the way I thought I would have in 2012.

When I started in 2009, I said 2012 would be my breakout year. That wasn't the case. I was very lazy. So my goals for the new year are relatively the same.

- Appearing on TV.
- Featuring or opening on the road for a name act.
- Recording my unofficial first special: A Number to A Name.

These goals along with a few others are attainable, just like they were last year. I just need to bust my butt this time.

JANUARY 4, 2013

I WAS BILLED as the headliner for a show at Coles of Houston on the north side of town. My good friend Adam Bob was also on the show, which was cool because I hadn't seen him on the scene for over a month. He had some new material that was nice. I had a decent set trying out some material that I had just written the day before, all of which I would say passed.

I credit my success to rehearsing the material, something I haven't done since my first few months of performing. Putting in the extra practice time helps on stage more so than just coming up with a premise and going right to the stage with it.

For the second time in a week I performed for forty plus minutes. This is a big deal for me because it used to be such a challenge for me to do twenty minutes. With that said, I've had a nice run the past two weeks. I featured on the road once, headlined in my city twice, and I put about $600 in my pocket, none of which I still have of course. I really need to fix this spending problem.

Anyway, before I go, I gotta give my congrats to my boy Ken. He's in Virginia featuring for Tony Rock. Ken, Adam Bob, Netra Babin, and I all started around the same time so it's always good to see success out of the class.

JANUARY 16, 2013

HELLO, Hello,

I feel good right now. Or at least I feel better than I felt earlier today. I was rather depressed, feeling like I just can't catch a break in this comedy game, not to mention that I just found out I was not selected to compete in the Laughing Skull Competition. I prayed on the matter. I prayed for a breakthrough or just something to motivate me to push harder. I may have already been granted my wish.

I finished reading *Last Words* by George Carlin this morning. So I went to Barnes & Nobles to pick up a book I had ordered a week ago. The name of the book is *The War of Art* by Steven Pressfield. It was recommended to me by Slade Ham. It's an amazing book and a super easy read. I'm already a third of the way through. It really speaks to artists and thoroughly explains how resistance gets the best of us when we are trying to work. The content of the book is very useful!

Aside from reading, I'm gearing up for two major moves. First, my fourth annual MickeyLodeon Fest. It will celebrate twenty-six years of living and four years of performing standup. Major move number two is, well, to literally move. My sights are set on Chicago. My girl wants to make it happen sooner than I intended. She's thinking October.

I'm thinking (gulp) so be it.

> The most important thing about art is to
> work. Nothing else matters except
> sitting down every day and trying. ~
>
> Steven Pressfield

FEBRUARY 25, 2013

HEY, folks. How are you? Me, I've been good myself. The past two weeks were great. I recently set a goal for myself to earn at least $800 a month in comedy, and I was able to do $1100 this month.

It started last weekend, which happened to be the weekend of Valentine's Day and the NBA All-Star Game, which was held in Houston this year. I had three paid gigs including two on Valentine's day. On Saturday the 16th, I was able to catch Shaq's All-Star Comedy Show. This came courtesy of Shawn Harris who hooked me and Ken up with tickets.

We were trying to get in free on the "hey, we're comedians" card, but security wasn't having it. Thankfully, Shawn happened to walk by and catch wind of our struggles. If there's one thing I can say about Shawn, it's that he will never leave you outside.

The show was awesome! It was my first time witnessing comedy inside a large arena. It was hosted by Bill Bellamy

(*Def Jam How to Be a Player, Who's Got Jokes*). I must give props to up and coming comedian Lavar Walker out of Atlanta. He is one of the newest members of the Shaq All Star Tour and he had a great set that night.

That weekend I received news that I would be featuring at the Improv for the first time. It would be the weekend following the All-Star Game, and I would be performing with Paul Mooney again. The last time Paul Mooney was in town I hosted the show and subsequently became acquainted with his road manager, Arrie. I gave her a call asking if I could work with Paul again and she granted me the wish. Making that call was a big accomplishment for me because I have a problem asking people for things, fearing that I'm being a bother.

So, the Paul Mooney weekend came around and it turned out fun for the most part. I had solid sets throughout the weekend, however there was a hiccup.

Since Thursday I had been running next door to Wal-Mart to buy plain white t-shirts for Paul to autograph for his fans. I was also accepting the $10 he charged for the signed t-shirts. In addition, Paul was taking pictures with the fans onstage and that is where the blunder took place.

I wasn't aware that he was also charging $10 for the pictures. So on Saturday, Paul felt that I was shorting him money. He had me hand the shirt-selling duties to one of the Improv staff members and ordered me off the stage. This occurred in the middle of handling customers so it was a tad embarrassing. I apologized later for the misunderstanding.

Other than getting accused of stealing by a legend, it was a good weekend. I feel good knowing and believing that more work is to come. Maybe not with Paul Mooney, but I'm certain there will be more.

More features. More opportunities. More chapters in my legacy to be written.

Here's another little nugget for young comedians from yours truly. If a headliner asks you to count the number of empty seats in a comedy club, do it.

After getting scolded by Paul, I approached him in the green room and apologized. He somewhat accepted it and made the request that I just mentioned. I had never been asked to do such a thing before and didn't think he seriously wanted to know the numbers. The crazy thing is I did in fact get the numbers of the empty seats. It was 96. However, I still felt uncomfortable about the mix-up that occurred, and I never reported the number to him, which was stupid because that may have been my saving grace. After all, I came into the weekend thinking I could become Paul's permanent feature.

10

A Little Bit of Everything

APRIL 2, 2013

IN THE COMEDY WORLD, just like in any other atmosphere, it's easy to allow jealousy to consume you. You and your peers are all fighting for a common goal and it sometimes appears they are closer to the prize than you are. You are happy for them, but don't quite understand why you aren't being granted the same opportunities. You feel you work just as hard as them, if not harder even. And sometimes, before you know it, a few fellows who have embarked on the journey after you are now getting some of the opportunities you desire.

It's not like I'm a slouch. People respect me and some would love to be in my position. So why don't I love my position? Why do I compare myself so much? If I were the only one doing what I do, would I still feel like I'm behind the curve? Most importantly, why can't I truly be happy for my colleagues and their achievements? After all, that's what I would want from them, to be happy for me.

Personally, I have endured darker days in battling this emotion. It visits me from time to time and has been popping up uninvited the past couple of weeks. Fortunately, I have been praying and reading, and by doing so I have been able to handle the emotion more maturely as of late and to be happy for my peers when they excel.

One book that has been very helpful is *Battlefield of the Mind* by Joyce Myers. It alerts you to certain mind traps that the Enemy tries to set up in your head to keep you thinking negatively. Myers advises to always think positively because positive thinking produces a positive way of living.

With a positive outlook on life I can be happy for my friends and siblings. The spotlight doesn't always have to be on me. When others excel in life I can be happy for them and know that their success doesn't make me a failure.

I recall my time at my first job when I was a bagger at Kroger. All my friends were soon promoted to cashier. I was the only one of my group that was still bagging groceries and collecting shopping carts from the parking lot. I was not happy at all, but I didn't openly complain. My patience would be rewarded when I was promoted to be a grocery stocker, which proved to be far more beneficial to me down the line than if I had been a cashier like the friends that I initially envied.

Though sometimes I may feel like I'm in last place, I'm sure it's nothing more than a silly lie that I temporarily allowed myself to believe. Maybe the position on hold for me requires a little more preparation time than usual. And if so, then I indeed have some work to do. And best believe I'm going to do it.

Thanks for letting me open up.

APRIL 24, 2013

I HAD A PRETTY COOL WEEKEND. Guy Torry (*American History X, Life*) was in town at the Houston Improv and I was hoping that I would get the nod to open for him. It was interesting because I'd been learning about the importance of trusting in God without wavering and believing He will do what you ask if you don't doubt and worry about it.

So when I emailed Raymond, the Improv manager, on Wednesday, which is two days after comedians are advised to do so, I put it in my head that I would not doubt or worry if I would get the call. Sure enough, I got the call later that day.

Guy Torry was real cool. He's the ultimate trash talker. He called me African so many times I began digging for answers on Ancestry. One of the coolest things about him is he likes to pray with the comedians before each show. He owns a comedy club in L.A. and told me I can work his room when I go out there next month. He also told me he would try to set me up on a showcase for the booker of the new season of ComicView. That would be incredible, since my written goal is to tape for TV this year.

I have a show coming up this Sunday. I'm producing it and I titled it "Housley in the House." I will attempt to do characters on stage, something I've never done on a show before. I told myself I wanted to sell fifty tickets to the show. So far I've personally sold two, but I'm keeping the faith. I'm heading out to promote as soon as I put this pen down.

I'm petrified of going up to people to make sales, but I did exactly that last night. I approached almost everybody in the comedy venue I attended. The results were satisfying. Tonight, however I must do even better.

MAY 4, 2013

THE "HOUSLEY IN THE HOUSE" show was a lot of fun. I said I wanted fifty people at the show and I got pretty close. I was only short thirty people. Despite the small attendance, the show was great. The crowd displayed high energy throughout the show. They were receptive to everyone who touched the stage. Ken Boyd co-hosted the show for me. This was so I could have time to change into my characters for the night.

I did two characters. Miguel the Poet and Sugar Bomb the Punkster. Miguel is a lady's man. His poetry is clever and extremely X-Rated. Sugar Bomb is a gay rapper. He is a gangster punk; therefore, he is referred to as the Punkster.

Even though he is openly gay, he warns against anyone tempted to make fun of his sexuality.

Both Miguel and Sugar Bomb went over well with the audience. Carl Hunter and Sandrell Ross both did their thing in ten-minute guest spots. Eddie B served as headliner for the show and he closed it out real strong.

Overall it was a great show in which I have no complaints. Well, I did lose money, but hey, it happens. Ken and I hung out after the show in what turned out to be an interesting night.

That was Sunday and today is Saturday so of course there is more to talk about. Tuesday I started rehearsals for a play I'm doing, *Too Funny to Be Forgotten*. The screenplay is put together by actress and entertainment attorney Jalene Mack. I'm essentially playing myself as an up and coming comedian—shouldn't be too hard.

In the play, I'm not very good at first, but after receiving visits from comedians like Richard Pryor and Moms Mabley, I learn how to really work a crowd. I'm currently going over my lines so I can be off book by the next rehearsal.

Right now, I am in Wilmington, NC for the Cape Fear Comedy Festival. I'm staying at the Extended Stay—a nice, small, chain hotel with reasonable rates. This is my first time doing a comedy festival. I have been here since Wednesday and it's been cool so far. I will share more details about the show tomorrow on the plane ride back to Houston. Otherwise, this would be a very long entry.

MAY 8, 2013

OK, so I'm a few days behind. I was supposed to talk about my trip to North Carolina for the Cape Fear Comedy Festival. Let me start by saying that I had a fun time.

I arrived in Wilmington around 2:00 p.m. coming off what had to be the smallest plane that Spirit Airlines possessed. I got off the drone and patiently waited for Matt Ward, one of the co-founders of the festival, to pick me up and take me to my hotel.

The festival utilized four venues to serve as performing grounds for the comics. Those venues were the Theater Act, The Bean Room, The Soapbox Lounge, and Nutt St. Comedy Room.

With Nutt St. being the lone actual comedy club, it was by far the premier stage of the quartet to showcase on. I was on the late show at the Soapbox, which was literally upstairs from Nutt St. The crowd was small, and I had an okay set at best, but hey, it was the first night so no big deal. Well, except for the part where I let all the comics leave before I realized I had no ride to my hotel. An hour-and-a-half long walk later, I was in bed, exhausted and finished with night one.

On Thursday afternoon, I ordered a pizza that would serve as my dinner for the rest of the week. Later that evening I was back at the Soapbox, and this time there was no crowd at all. All the performers were tacked on to the end of the two shows downstairs at Nutt St. I was the very last comedian of the night to perform, which was kind of cool to me. What's even cooler is that I got a ride home that night. Thanks, Dusty Slay!

Friday night was fun. I went for some pre-show ice cream with Luke Thayer and a comedienne whose name I don't recall. Then it was time for my scheduled set at Nutt St. I had to follow a big ball of energy in Jared Logan. And I mean a BIG ball of energy. He had the crowd in a frenzy. I went up, brought the crowd to my level, and delivered perhaps my best performance of the weekend. The great night was capped off by a ride home. Thanks, Greg Williams!

Saturday night would be the finale. I was scheduled at the Soapbox once again, meaning I never set foot in either the Theater Act or the Bean Room. Unlike the first two nights, the Soapbox was packed. Oh, and if by now you're thinking that the Soapbox sounds like a laundromat, well that's because it is. When you walk into the bar you can see a room in the very back loaded with washers and dryers.

I proceeded to have a solid set, and afterwards I was lavished with some high praise, which came courtesy of Timmy Sherrill. He's the co-founder of the festival and the owner of The Nutt St. Comedy Room. He told me that out of sixty-five comedians I was the stand out performer. What a delight that was to hear. But what was even more delightful was that...

I got a ride home. Thanks Derrick!

MAY 11, 2013

YESTERDAY I PERFORMED the lead role in the stage play *Too Funny to Be Forgotten*. It went over well. The whole cast worked together to put on a strong performance. Thomas Miles, better known as Nephew Tommy from the *Steve Harvey Morning Show*, was in attendance and he spoke very highly of the play. Jalene Mack is pushing to get it picked up and ran through the college circuit.

That would be incredible!

MAY 16, 2013

IT'S 9:24 A.M. (Pacific time)

I'm at the Oakland airport waiting on my homie and fellow comedian Canice Nnana to pick me up. I'm out here to do the Bay Area Comedy Competition for the second year in a row. I'm winning this thing. Mark my words.

This trip has already come with its share of adversity. I flew from Houston to Dallas where I had a four-hour layover. That layover would turn to eight hours when most of the planes entering town were delayed due to tornados that struck a town southwest of Dallas. I didn't get to Oakland until 4:00 a.m.

It's 9:34 a.m.

I just finished a nice breakfast, so I feel pretty good at the moment. However, something happened earlier this morning that left me rather perplexed.

I was reading my Bible, and when I finished, I set it down in the seat next to me. This lady approached me a short while later, picked up my Bible, and slammed it in my lap saying, "Hey, read this." She then stormed off before I could react. I couldn't even really comprehend what had just happened. It was disrespectful, but I suppose there are worse things that could've happened. Nonetheless I prayed for the lady. It was either that or chase her down. I opted to pray.

It's 9:44 a.m.

Where art thou Canice?

MAY 19, 2013

IT'S SUNDAY. The last day of competition for the Bay Area Comedy Festival. The semifinals start at 7:00 p.m. and the finals start at 9:30 p.m.

I will start going over my material very soon. Unfortunately, I won't be using any of it tonight because I didn't advance. Had you going, huh?!?

There were four preliminary rounds. Two shows on both Friday and Saturday at 8:00 and 10:30. I did the 10:30 show on Friday. My heat featured nineteen comedians. That's three more than the 8:00 show on Saturday, which featured the second most comedians. No excuses, however.

I had a good set so I can't complain. The comedians that did advance were all worthy.

Okay, I just thought of a cool way to end this entry. Of the sixteen comedians in the semifinals, six will advance to the finals. I will list the names of who I believe will advance tonight and I will inform who the actual qualifiers were in the next entry. So without further ado:

Antoine Scott	Rip Michaels
Marc Henderson	Noah Gardenswartz
Matt Rife	Jay Rich

I'll take Antoine Scott as the overall winner.

MAY 19, 2013 - Later that night

SO I ENDED up going 3 for 6 in my predictions for the finals in the Bay Area Comedy Competition. The finalists were Rip Michaels, Matt Rife, Jay Rich, Kevin Tate, Skills Hudson and Justin Lucas. Rip Michaels took home the crown and $5,000. I guess it was a bit of redemption for him. Legend has it that he would've won last year had he not gone over the allotted ten minutes.

Now that the competition is over, everyone is headed back to their hometowns. I, on the other hand, am headed to L.A. What awaits me there? Who knows. Admittedly, I'm nervous about going, but that must be the Enemy trying to scare me away from something good. There's only one way to find out.

L.A., see you tonight.

MAY 20, 2013

I'VE BEEN in Los Angeles for about eight hours so far, and I've spent about six of those hours walking. I took the Megabus here from Oakland. A young lady I met on the bus helped point me in the right direction to North Holly-wood where I would be staying with fellow comedian Crystal Powell. However, it was late when I arrived in L.A. so I missed the last bus to North Hollywood.

After waiting at the bus stop for an hour, I decided to embark on a ten-mile journey. I had to cross a plethora of bums and walk by freeways with no sidewalk. What's worse is that Crystal is not home. So I am currently at a McDonalds writing, which reminds me—I think I stumbled across a surefire bit last night about homeless people. If so, "the walk" might have been worth it after all.

MAY 26, 2013

I HAVE BEEN in L.A. for almost a week now. And what a week it has been. Let's break it down by day.

Monday – I rode the Megabus for the first time from Oakland to Los Angeles. I arrived in L.A. at 12:30 a.m. so I guess what happened next should belong to Tuesday, but I'll stay put for now. I'm supposed to travel to North Hollywood to stay with a fellow comedian. However, I missed the last bus to North Hollywood. At 2:30 a.m. I began walking.

Tuesday – I arrived at my destination at 7:00 a.m. My comedian friend would not be home for the day. So, I spent the bulk of the day walking up and down Lankershim Blvd. I stumbled across Ha Ha's Comedy Cafe. The timing was perfect because they were just starting their open mic. I signed up, had a nice set, and got booked to do a show there on the upcoming Monday.

Wednesday – At 4:30 a.m. I awoke because it's not easy sleeping on a park bench, and I had a random text message from Billy Sorrells. Billy had moved to L.A. a year ago after garnering some attention after one of his YouTube videos went viral. I called him and told him my situation. He gave me his address and I crashed on his couch that morning.

Thursday – After a good night's rest at a hotel that Sandrell booked for me for the next 3 days, I went and checked out the Comedy Store. The Comedy Store is cool, and it had multiple showrooms inside the one building. I caught two different shows in the same room—The C-Word show and then right afterwards, the Crack'em Up Thursdays show. At the second show, I was able to watch Keenan and Damon Wayans work out new material.

Friday – I went to the Comedy Union and caught a show that featured Sydney Castillo, Tiffany Haddish, and a few others. I saw Guy Torry who showed a lot of love. However, he couldn't grant me the stage time he promised me a month ago when I opened for him in Houston.

Saturday – Aww, the infamous Saturday night. I will keep this one brief. I hung out with my cousin Troy in Santa Monica and had one heck of a time. We hit a couple of clubs, had drinks, and didn't make it back to his apartment until 3:00 a.m. He had to be to work at 6:00 a.m. Thanks to his girlfriend, Angel, who is such a sweetheart, he made it to work.

So that was my first week in Los Angeles. Paraphrased a bit, but you get the gist.

Week Two here I come!

In case you're wondering, my friend Crystal was out of town when I initially arrived in L.A. I was without a place to stay and spent my first two nights on the street. I cried like a baby that second night. Being homeless is a skill. In due time, Crystal made it back to L.A. and my stay with her was pleasant. Staying at her place also helped me get over my fear of puppies. She had two of them.

P.S. Comics, if you're ever in L.A. for some extended time, sign up with Central Casting. It's a service that helps you book gigs as an extra for sitcoms and movies. It's a good way to put some cash in your pocket during the day.

MAY 30, 2013

I RECEIVED some high praise from a prominent figure in

comedy the other night. I went to the famous Hollywood Laugh Factory to catch a show that Tony Rock was hosting. I had spoken to him earlier in the day, and he mentioned he would get me some stage time.

I arrived at the Laugh Factory forty-five minutes early and waited for Tony to pull up. When he arrived, he talked to a girl at the front door and found out that the owner of the club, Jamie Masada, was in the showroom. Tony immediately rushed in the showroom as I follow close behind.

"I'm going to get you a showcase right now," he tells me.

He greeted Jamie who was sitting down watching and observing the young comics on stage. Tony urged Jamie to give me 3 minutes of stage time. After debating with himself for a moment, Jamie agreed.

Less than two minutes later I was called to the stage. I went on nervous as hell, which Tony later told me that he noticed. I stumbled over jokes, but through it all I was able to get laughs once the punchlines landed. After the show, all of the comedians were called upstairs to meet with Jamie for his opinion of our sets.

When it was my turn to speak with Jamie, he had nothing but kind words for me. He told me I was the only one that physically made him laugh. He said he wanted me on his six to eight-minute showcase and if I nailed it, I could soon be a regular at the club. It was so awesome. Thank you, Jesus!

Oh, and I must tell you about the night before the Laugh Factory show. I did my show at Ha Ha's Comedy Cafe. I had to bring five people to the show but being from out of town I didn't really know anyone. However, I was able to get three people to come. I had just met them an hour before the show at a Starbucks. In addition to that, I ended up having a great set, which took place right before Damon Wayans hit the stage. He acknowledged my set on stage and gave me props after the show.

After all that, I am left with three more days of the Cali experience. We'll see what it offers.

I had a hard time coming up with a title for this chapter because of the events that took place in the given time frame. There were good moments (travel). And there were bad moments (jealousy, homeless-ness). I had no such trouble with the next chapter. I dealt with death, missed opportunities, and irresponsibility. And oh yeah …. infidelity.

11

Who Doesn't Like a Little Drama?

JUNE 3, 2013

ON JUNE 1, 2013 my friend and fellow comedian Toucheé Jackson passed away from a heart attack. The more I think about it, the more I realize how much I'm going to miss the man. "Little Mickey" is what he used to always call me. It was his own way of ribbing me about looking like I was from Africa.

I met Toucheé four years ago at Tyme Square. I had only been doing comedy for two weeks when I watched him perform; I thought he was so cool. The best thing about that night was that he gave me (a new comedian who he had just met) his number.

He then told me if I ever wanted to write with him to just call. Mind you, he was a professional comedian with about seven or eight years of experience. That blew my mind and made me feel good at the same time. I never called to write, but I used that number several times to have him headline some shows I produced in the years to come.

While I was still less than a year in, Toucheé would often invite me to his comedy rooms where he held open mic nights. He always ran a fun room, and I always felt comfortable performing at his rooms. I mention this because in my first year my performances were so hit-or-miss. It was at one of Toucheé weekly shows, Zona Latina, where I would gain the confidence needed to be consistently funny.

Toucheé was also the first person to have me host his show. There's so much more I could say about this man, but for now my brother, Rest in Peace. Much love my friend. Hold it down in Heaven. "Little Mickey" will hold it down for you here.

JUNE 5, 2013

THE HOUSTON IMPROV served as the host venue for ComicView auditions on June 3rd and 4th. Most comedians on the showcases started getting their call to perform on the 30th or 31st of May. I got my call three hours before the first showcase. Talk about having faith. While I was quite surprised that I was overlooked, I never got down about not being picked to showcase, nor did I doubt I would get picked. It was a great feeling, and I had a superb set at the showcase. Now I must practice the same faith and believe that I'll get selected to tape for ComicView in Atlanta. Admittedly, it's been a little harder to do than usual. I've been just too excited.

After my audition set for ComicView, people approached me with congratulations. I did well, and I believed I had a great chance of being selected to tape. However, only one comedian was selected from Houston. There were various theories as to why that was, and we'll probably never know the true reason. At the time, this was my best shot at making television, and I struck out. The sting was real.

JUNE 17, 2013

IT'S Monday night and I'm in the house. I might as well write. This past weekend I hosted for comedian Bruce Bruce (former Host of BET's *ComicView*) at the Improv. I got a pretty good workout by doing seven shows in three nights. Two on Friday and Sunday, and three on Saturday.

On Friday night, I made a big mistake. I was asked to close out each show, which is what the host normally does anyway. Bruce Bruce's road manager, Skee, gave me a specific spiel to announce to the audience after each show. I did it correctly after the first show. However, on the second show, I didn't make the specific announcements at all because when Bruce finished his set, I was nowhere to be found. I wasn't even in the building; I was outside in my car charging my phone.

When I decided to head back in, I began to worry as I saw people walking out to their cars. My fears were confirmed when two girls stopped me and said, "Hey! Bruce Bruce was looking for you."

I was so embarrassed. I ran back into the Improv and waited for Bruce to finish taking pictures with fans. As soon as he was done, I quickly apologized. He showed no signs of being offended and told me everything was all good. (The guy is very nice by the way). Skee, however, warned me not to let it happen again.

I made sure it didn't.

JUNE 24, 2013

I AM IN NEW YORK, New York. Brooklyn to be exact. I drove the twenty-five hours here from Houston with Ken. He had been planning to move here for over a year, and the time had finally arrived. This marks the first time I've ever set foot in the Big Apple.

We arrived in New York around 9:00 p.m. last night. We checked into the hotel and immediately went back out to meet our guy Kevin Iso. Coincidently, Kevin also moved to New York from Houston less than a week ago. He was at a spot called the Knitting Factory where the comedy is normally hosted by Hannibal Burress. Hannibal wasn't there last night so another guy served as host. It was a cool show, but we were only observers.

Tonight however, we were performers. Ken and I were informed of a spot called Visions. It's hosted by comedian Brooklyn Mike. He put us both in the lineup as well as comedian Stacy Anderson. Stacy is originally from New York but currently lives in Houston where she also started performing. The three of us served as the H-Town portion of the show, and we all held it down. Philadelphia comedian TuRae Gordon was the headliner. He was great, and he showed us a lot of love after the show.

Well, I leave in the morning. It's been a trip with its share of drama. Ken is essentially homeless, and I am essentially single. I got caught cheating the night before I left for New York, and it has been like hell since. So I've had to deal with the consequences of a foolish act while away.

I'll probably detail that story more in depth twenty years from now when I write a "tell all" book. For now, deuces— to this entry and to New York.

Until next time.

Due to the circumstances, I didn't get to enjoy New York as much as I could've. There was a city closer to home, however, that I would come to enjoy very much.

12

Everybody Loves Austin, TX

AUGUST 17, 2013

I'M CURRENTLY high off a great moment that occurred last night. I headlined out of town for the first time in my young comedy career.

The setting was Austin, TX at JaeAndrea's Hair Salon. Yes, a hair salon. It was a very nice hair salon and the place was packed. The show was put on by comedian/actor Aaron Spivey-Sorrells. He saw me perform at the Houston Improv a few months back and determined I would be great for his room. What an honor, and what a time I had.

Outside of the show having a tad too many comedians, it was dope. I went onstage with energy, I improvised well, and I performed for about forty-five minutes. I sold some merchandise and it felt cool that the newer comedians knew who I was even though we had never met. I was happy that my brothers both rode to Austin with me and that my sister came from her school, Texas State University, in nearby San Marcos, TX.

All in all, I had a great time in Austin, and I hope there are many more headlining gigs to come.

AUGUST 24, 2013

GOOD MORNING! The past two days I have been waking up early to work on my material. I feel really good because it's something I've been trying to do for a while, but I could never manage to string two days in a row together. However, I did today, and the dedication to writing and rehearsing daily is paying off. I feel comfortable on stage, and I feel like I have a lot more freedom within my sets.

Another cool thing is that I've been able to do shows where I can be on stage for twenty-five plus minutes at a time. Ali Siddiq helped me write a few jokes with more of a conversational flow rather than my usual setup, punch line style. The conversational style allows me to be more personal and it also provides the potential for longer and stronger bits. So the extended stage time provides good practice for that.

The real reason I wrote this entry is because I forgot to note that I appeared on TV on Monday. It wasn't national TV, that's been ever so elusive thus far. Yet it was significantly better than anything I've previously done on the tube. I was on Comcast Sports Net on a show titled *Sports Talk Live Houston*. I was being interviewed by sports broadcaster Kevin Eschenfelder who does the halftime shows for the Houston Rockets. I almost missed my spot, however.

I was running late due to heavy traffic that I underestimated. I made it just in time. When I appeared on TV, I had been in the building less than two minutes. Thankfully I made it because I was able to promote a show I had at the Improv on the 22nd. It was such a cool experience for me. What made it even cooler was when I did the Improv show, a group approached me afterwards and told me they decided to come after seeing me on Comcast.

Sweet!

SEPTEMBER 22, 2013

I WENT TO AUSTIN, TX yesterday along with Sandrell to showcase for NBC's Standup Diversity. This was the fourth year that I did the showcase and the first time I advanced to the second round. In fact, it was the first time I advanced to the second round in a national competition ever.

The judges only picked four comics out of twenty-five in my heat. I went last, and the judges mistakenly dismissed the comics before I performed. I had to remind them that I hadn't yet performed and the judges got a good laugh out of that. They made everyone sit down, and I proceeded to tell my jokes. I did my material about my struggles as a skinny man, and it went over very well.

The judges posted the names of the comics they wanted to see do a two-minute set. It felt so good to see my name on that paper. At the conclusion of the second round, I learned I wasn't selected for the final showcase, but I was happy nonetheless. It was encouraging to advance.

I'm beginning to feel like Austin is my city. Last month, I headlined out of town for the first time. This month, I made it to the second round in a national showcase for the first time.

In Austin!

OCTOBER 14, 2013

THE LAST TIME I wrote in this journal I had just left Austin, TX, and that is where I find myself now. I had a show last night at a church in San Antonio. It was cool because my grandma Beulah came to check me out, which she has done several times before. Sometimes she'll even travel with my sister to catch my shows in Houston.

The show was put together by Nigerian Comedian MC PC who also lives in Houston. He has a great vision of a show and movement titled the "Be Yourself Comedy Show" that he is touring in churches across various cities. The show features comedy, poetry, and live music.

One of the comedians featured was a guy from Lagos,

Nigeria named Lafup. It was his first time in the states. He was good too. I didn't understand all his material but the Nigerians at the church were cracking up the whole time. There was a girl that performed praise dancing to a powerful sermon rather than a song. She was very good as well. It was a good show despite starting two hours late.

The night before, I performed for a Hispanic audience, which is always fun. This made two shows in a row where I was the only African American comedian on a show. With Austin being only an hour away from San Antonio, my girl and I decided to hit a few open mics away from home.

I feel good right now. At the beginning of October, I challenged myself to write every day for the entire month. I call it the Halloween Challenge. My goal was to complete a book which will also be titled *The Halloween Challenge*. There's no chance I'm going to finish by Halloween, but the neat thing is I feel like I'm capable of writing until I complete the book, whether it takes two months or two years. It's like once you discipline yourself to do something daily, you activate dormant abilities that you had all along. The discipline of writing and hitting stages daily is going to help me down the line.

On Thursday, I'm hosting a show at Texas Southern University for their Homecoming week. I'll be performing with BET comedian Tyler Craig. I'll also be getting paid $500, which will be the most I've ever been paid for a single show. Praise!

2013 was coming to a close. It had been a good year up to that point and would get better before it ended.

13

The End...I Think

NOVEMBER 19, 2013

FOR MONTHS I had been trying to achieve a goal I set for myself to write forty jokes and perform thirty times in one month. I was finally able to perform thirty times on stage in October. I'm still pushing for the forty jokes. I also set a goal for myself to begin a book and write for thirty days straight. I accomplished that feat as well. The thirty days of writing enabled me to complete the first two chapters of *The Halloween Challenge*.

November has been no slouch either. I started the month by featuring at the Joke Joint Comedy Showcase. It gave me a chance to do thirty minutes several times. I also told jokes at a boxing match at TSU during that same weekend. I was informed a few days ago that I will be competing in the Funniest Comic in Texas Competition. This is gratifying because I remember being upset that I wasn't picked to participate in it last year.

November got even better yesterday when Tony Rock asked me to hit the road and perform with him in Dallas, Texas. Dallas has two Improv Comedy Clubs located in nearby suburbs of the city. One is in Arlington and the other in Addison. I've been trying to perform in one of them for the longest time. Now I can scratch that off my bucket list as I will be performing at both. The Funniest Comic in Texas Competition is held at the Addison Improv and I'll be opening for Tony Rock at the Arlington Improv.

That means I can also cross "performing on the road with a national headliner" off the list.

NOVEMBER 25, 2013

SLEEPY, Sleepy, Sleepy. And with good reason. I've made four trips up and down Interstate 45, running between Houston and Dallas, and I still have two more trips to go. Tomorrow I must go back to Dallas for my preliminary round of the Funniest Comic in Texas Competition.

The previous trips to Dallas were a by-product of being able to feature for Tony Rock at the Arlington Improv. It would have been nice to have just stayed in Dallas from Thursday to Tuesday. However, my job wasn't too thrilled about me leaving the grocery store the weekend before

Thanksgiving. I compromised a bit and offered to work a half day on Saturday.

Here's how it played out. After the show Friday night, I hung out with Tony. I dropped him off at the hotel around four in the morning and left for Houston right after getting to work at 8:00 a.m. After working for about five hours, I clocked out and was soon back on the I-45 arriving in Dallas at 6:00 p.m.—just in time for the 7:00 p.m. show.

I was up for thirty-six hours without sleep, and eight of those hours were spent behind the wheel. Bananas! But you know what? It's all about the hustle, and it was a great weekend. But for now, I just want to go to bed.

NOVEMBER 29, 2013

ON TUESDAY NOVEMBER 28TH, I competed in the Funniest Comic in Texas Competition. I was in the first preliminary round of eight comedians. The top two comedians advanced, and no, I wasn't one of the two. However, I had fun and I believe I will be booked more in Dallas because of the contest.

The following night, something else cool happened. Dejuan performed standup comedy for the first time. It was on open mic night at a bar called Bier Haus, which usually has a fun and energetic audience. I was asked to host the show maybe fifteen minutes before it started—meaning that the first person to introduce my brother on stage as a standup comic was his brother, me! How awesome is that?!?

He asked me to introduce him as D.J. Housley. He did okay for it being his first time. He talked about our dad and our Uncle Derrick. He sprinkled in a few jokes about roaches for good measure. He was excited afterwards that he finally did it. He was also thankful to Sandrell for signing his name on the list even though she did it against his will.

After just one set, he is already talking about tours and sitcoms. He is really buying big into this life as a comedian, and I can't blame him. I was the same way. You all read my first entries.

Dejuan loved doing standup, but he didn't push it as hard as he would've liked to. There were several factors hindering his devotion to the art ranging from his job to family and more. Eventually, Dejuan rededicated his life to Christ and found it too difficult to balance comedy with the work that he was called to carry out for the Lord. After a year, he put comedy on the back burner; a decision I truly admired him for.

DECEMBER 31, 2013

IT'S the last day of the year. In my opinion, 2013 has flown by very swiftly, however, not without its share of adversity and triumph. Every year, people picture what their year is going to look like. For me 2013 was the closest I have ever been to that mental picture.

I always wanted 2012 to be my year, and it didn't really go as planned. However, 2013 cleaned up some of 2012's loose ends. I wrote many more jokes this year, which strengthened my set overall. I headlined out of town for the first time. I performed at my first festival in North Carolina. I finally made it out of the prelims in a national showcase. I featured for two nationally known headliners, and I finally performed and got paid at an Improv other than the one in my backyard.

I competed in the Funniest Comic in Texas Competition, which was originally a goal for 2012 by the way. I stayed in L.A. for two weeks, in which the first two days I spent homeless. I visited New York for the first time, and I started working at Kroger—Again.

Well that's most of the important stuff for now. If something else jumps out at me, I'll add it in as I write. Anyhow, 2014 is about seventeen hours away. I thank God I am able to see another year. I want to spend this upcoming year working hard and being happy. (Just remembered that I starred in a play this year and was offered a role in a local movie a couple of weeks ago). I've already written down my goals for the year. Now it's about executing the plan— staying focused, reading more, minimizing distractions, believing more, and not doubting myself so much.

2014 awaits. Chicago awaits. My national television debut awaits.

Before I go. Congrats to my girl, Sandrell Ross, for graduating from college at the University of Houston Downtown. That reminds me. School awaits. Or does it just wait? I don't know, we'll see. Happy New Year, folks.

Hoping your 2014 is as promising as mine will be. Please pray and put God first in your lives. Don't be pressured or stressed by the world.

Work Hard and Be Happy!

Mickey Housley

JANUARY 14, 2014

AH! It's the first entry of a new year. As I stated before, 2013 was a good year, but I don't want to get complacent. The 2014 plan is to continue to work hard and monitor the results as the year goes on.

Two weeks in and I feel I have been diligent, but there is room for improvement. I need to record myself more as well as write and book myself more. I need to complete assignments more efficiently. I'll come up with an idea and before I know it a month has passed before I take any action.

Two weeks in and there have been some cool moments already though. I hosted at the Improv this past week for John Reep. You may remember him from some Dodge truck commercials asking, "Does that thing got a Hemi in it?" Very cool guy I might add. Prior to this weekend, I had only opened for black comedians at the Improv, so it was nice showing the staff that I can work multiple demographics.

Two weeks in and I am assured this will be a great year.

MARCH 6, 2014

HAPPY BIRTHDAY, grandpa Joshua. He would have turned eighty-seven today. It's a little ironic to me that after a month of no journal entries, the day I finally decide to write is on my grandpa's birthday. The irony is in the fact that the first thing I was going to write about was my birthday.

I think of how my grandpa, who passed away seven years ago, never got to witness his grandson as an entertainer. I think he would have been proud. Maybe not too proud. His dream was for me to play in the NBA for the San Antonio Spurs. Fortunately, for the Spurs, they decided not to draft me.

For the past few years I have had some success producing my annual MickeyLodeon Fest celebrating my birthday and comedy anniversary. This will be the fifth installment. The first two were at a bar (Yum Yums) and the third and fourth shows were at a banquet hall (The Palm Palace). This one will be at an actual comedy club: The Joke Joint Comedy Showcase.

I have a stacked show that includes several guest performances. It will be headlined by TuRae Gordon. I am quite proud of myself for putting this show together. With the help of social media and friends, I have built a legitimate buzz for the show. It has the potential to be my biggest show to date. I'm excited because I have big plans for the MickeyLodeon Fest in the near and distant futures.

MARCH 13, 2014

YES! Finally, a chance to sit back and reflect.

MickeyLodeon 5 is now four days passed. I would have to say it was a success and that I am happy. That is not to say, however, that it wasn't met with its share of challenges.

It started when I found out that I had to work on the day of the show. This was disappointing considering that I'm usually off on Sundays. I also had to shoot my part in an upcoming movie titled *Live, Love, Laugh* that morning. Working made filming my scene a bit challenging as well. I got it done, nonetheless, and I'm excited because it's my first movie.

Thankfully my boss arranged for me to only work a few hours. However, those few hours of work prevented me from getting a haircut and buying new clothes. I didn't go on stage as the man I envisioned.

Working the day-of also nearly caused a panic attack as I was forced to have Sandrell pick up TuRae from the airport. As it got close to his arrival time, I called Sandrell to see where she was. No matter how many times I called she would not answer her phone, which was uncharacteristic of her. I called TuRae and learned that she had indeed picked him up and they were on their way to get me.

We arrived at the Comedy Club about forty-five minutes before showtime and began to set up. Forty-five minutes later, I began to have a second, near panic attack. On every one of the three hundred tickets I sold or gave away, the start of the show clearly stated 7:00 p.m. The problem was that there was literally one person in the audience at the stated time. This was especially embarrassing because I told Rachel, the general manager of the Joke Joint Comedy Showcase, that I was expecting two hundred people.

I knew folks would be running late, but I didn't expect it to be the entire audience. I ran out to my car to pray, and before I knew it, a tear (or eight) ran down my cheek. I haven't told anybody the crying part of this story so let's keep that between us. I worked very hard for this show. I poured my heart and soul into it getting rid of every ticket. I spent close to $1,500 so for there to only be one person in the building at the start time was extremely painful.

However, soon enough people began to trickle in. I started at 7:30 p.m. Adam Bob hosted the first half of the show. He introduced all my comedians doing guest spots: Marcellus Crayton, Sandrell Ross, Mike Worm, Bob Morrissey, DJ Housley and Jaffer Khan. He also brought up Leroy who performed and then introduced me to the stage.

I did my thang for a few minutes and then introduced my boy Jay Hanna from New York, and then lastly TuRae who absolutely killed it. Singer Otecia Redman closed the show.

All in all, it was a great show. My mother was in attendance, making it the first time she had ever came to one of my shows. I received positive feedback from her and others over the next couple of days which is what anyone wants to hear. MickeyLodeon 5 will go down as one of my two favorites for now, but I have big plans for the upcoming festivities. You'll see!

Before I go, I would like to leave a lesson I learned: Do your best to stay calm when facing adversity. I was very disappointed with myself when the day was done because of how I reacted whenever something appeared to not go my way. I had to ask God for forgiveness because my actions showed little faith.

At the end of the day, regardless of how bleak things looked, everything I needed done was taken care of. I shot my part for the movie. TuRae got picked up from the airport. I arrived at my show on time. And I had a decent turnout. So besides adding a few wrinkles to my forehead, what did I accomplish by stressing?

Just some food for thought.

MARCH 15, 2014

SO, look at me. A five-year comedy veteran. I really don't like to use that word because five years is very young in comedy years. But it's cool when I consider the time or two I thought about quitting to know that I hung in.

One thing you learn when you become a comedian is that it is really hard work. It's truly nowhere near as easy as it looks. It takes being responsible and having discipline. It requires you to get up and write material when you don't feel like it. You must email comedy clubs for work and follow up even though you're afraid of rejection.

I don't watch a lot of television, but sometimes I see things that get me motivated. Of course, five years ago, it was the Kevin Garnett documentary that motivated me to search the internet for a place to perform standup for the first time. Something similar happened when I got home from work a few hours ago.

While I couldn't wait to get home and write, there was a documentary on former American Idol winner Ruben Studdard on TV that held my attention. Ruben admitted that he didn't work as hard as he should have early in his career. A colleague of Ruben's confirmed as much, stating that to make it in the industry you must love your craft more than anything. You can't be hung up trying to hang out all the time or allowing so many things to distract you. Focus is an area where I can use a major tune-up.

Another thing that always encourages me is when I see my comedian buddies doing good things. After the Ruben Studdard documentary, I saw three comedians I know personally on TV. Ali Siddiq, Billy Sorrells and Sleezy Evans. When you see people you know doing well, it helps bring your own dream closer to reality. It feels more attainable. But you must work for it.

If I sound a bit sentimental, perhaps it's because I always get that way around my anniversary. Another reason is because I've decided that this will be my last entry. Sure, it would be nice to keep writing until I record my first Show-time special or score a big box office hit, but five years feels like a good place to close. I'm fresh off my 5th Mickey-Lodeon Fest and a really good year. I'm content.

I thank God for giving me the idea to write a journal to chronicle my journey as a standup comedian. That is simply amazing to me. I hope that anyone who one day reads these entries will enjoy it and find it intriguing to get an up close view of the highs and lows a comedian goes through early in his or her career—The laughter and the tears that take place when going from a number to a name.

SPOILER ALERT – **I wrote more entries.**

14

Moving to Chicago

MARCH 20, 2014

WELL, that didn't take long.

When I first started writing, these entries were very short because I had a small notepad and I would only write enough to fill one page. Also, I was really honest. Not saying that I lie or exaggerate any of my stories, but the difference was that in the beginning I didn't have intentions of getting my journal published. So, when I wrote, it didn't feel as if I was writing to potential readers. It's like I was just speaking to myself. (Me just having an internal conversation.)

If I wanted to write about how much I disliked someone, I could do that. Not saying I did that, but hopefully you get my point. At the time, my decision to write a journal was only to have a personal chronicle of my ride to whatever success I attained.

Somewhere along the way I made the decision to one day publish the journal. For the longest time, I told myself that I would like to release the book when I performed on TV for the first time. After a while, I guess I got impatient. I decided that with or without the TV credit the time is now. So a few days ago I wrote what I thought was going to be the last entry for the book and what I'm writing now would be the first entry to the sequel.

However, as I began to type my entries, I realized I was missing the notebook that contained the bulk of my writings. That revelation was not a fun moment for me. This comes a week after I lost one of the notebooks I was using to write *The Halloween Challenge*. It was intended to be twenty chapters long and I was missing the first six.

I feel as though God was teaching me a lesson through this adversity. For starters, I need to keep up with my tablets. Also, perseverance. In the past this would be too big a blow and too discouraging for me to continue writing. But that's exactly what I've decided to do. Both books will get published. Hopefully I can publish *The Halloween Challenge this year*, and my journal in maybe another five or ten years. It's probably still a little too early for this book. It's like a music artist scoring two hit songs and then thinking it's time to make a greatest hits album.

Crazy right?

I thought that "The Halloween Challenge" would be my first book published. Instead it sits in my computer collecting cyber dust while patiently awaiting completion. I'm roughly 80% finished, but I haven't touched it in years nor am I in any rush to do so. Perhaps someday I'll finish it.

APRIL 10, 2014

SO APPARENTLY THERE is a rumor that got back to a nationally-known comedian that I don't "care for his comedy." I have the utmost respect for the person I anonymously speak of, as a person and comedian. The man has been nothing but nice to me and genuine from day one. His bit about Charles Ramsey, the man who rescued the three girls that were kidnapped in Ohio for ten years, is currently the funniest bit from any comedian to me.

That being said, I made a foolish mistake of admitting to someone that I wasn't the biggest fan prior to seeing his live show. It was an opinion that I formed after only seeing his standup on TV once. As a comedian, I believe that you don't get to see how good someone really is until you see them live. TV and radio don't always do an artist justice. I've felt the same way about plenty of artist including myself. When I look at myself recorded, I always feel like I'm lacking energy or I don't sound sharp.

I was disappointed to learn that the comments I made a few years ago were perceived and conveyed as I don't "mess" with the guy. Who am I to come to his show and publicly bash him?

I do believe things happen for a reason. There was a lesson

to be learned from the situation, which is to always speak well of people no matter what. There was a gentleman I met once, back when I was in network marketing by the name of Paul. All of his friends admired him because they never heard him say a bad thing about anyone. Never! He always spoke well of people even when they weren't around.

I slip from time to time, but I try to emulate that habit because words are powerful. Words can give life to people as easily as they can kill their spirits. And you never know what someone else may find offensive, regardless if you intended it to be offensive or not.

The situation honestly bothered me, but I'm always man enough to apologize when I'm wrong. I reached out to both the national comedian and the gentleman who mentioned my comments to him. Everything is cool. I have much love for both these guys and every one of my funny comrades. This is a grind and we all know it. Let's lift each other up and make the world laugh.

I couldn't remember Paul's last name, so I did some digging. Not only did I learn his last name, but I learned that he was involved in a lengthy affair with another man's wife. Sheesh. There's no way this guy didn't speak bad of anyone else. You can't have sex with a lady and not talk about her husband. It's egotistically impossible. And yeah, yeah, I know. I'm talking about someone. I told you I slip sometimes.

JUNE 20, 2014

I'M a few hours away from heading to Chicago. A move my fiancé and I have been planning for months now. We left Houston on Wednesday and stopped in Dallas that night to do an open mic at the Arlington Improv. We spent most of Thursday on the road before finally stopping in St. Louis to do some open mics there as well.

We are still in St. Louis debating whether we should do some sightseeing or just shoot to Chicago. There's a place here called Fitzgerald's that has the best pizza. That would be my biggest reason for staying.

The Tuesday before we left Houston was cool as I was able to perform standup for a show that is to be televised. I was picked to film for the show by legendary Houston comedian Juan Villareal who is the host and producer of the show. He saw me perform for the first time very recently. He liked my set, and before you know it I was added to his lineup to tape!

Juan and his team of producers shopped their show "Only Juan" to several television networks, however they have yet to find a taker. One more roadblock on the path to Comic Greatness.

AUGUST 4, 2014

IT'S AMAZING how long I go sometimes between entries. I can't believe I've been in Chicago for over a month and this is the first time I'm writing about it. Where should I begin?

I really like this city. I haven't done anything special, but just being here is cool to me. The move itself is an accomplishment.

Being from Houston, I grew accustomed to the big city feel. I always told myself even before comedy that if I ever moved I would go to Chicago. And what do you know? Here I am. It's still warm here, so who knows what I'll be writing a month from now.

The Chicago comedy scene is nice. There are more places to hone my skills here than back home. In fact, Chicago has more open mics on a Monday than Houston has all week. You can hit 3 or 4 on a given night, but you might have to walk a bit because parking is a drag.

I am not the man out here (nor was I in Houston for that matter). In a sense, I'm starting over. There are longer waits to go on stage and no more free entry at the comedy clubs. You can get spoiled by your home scene after a while. Yet I embrace the challenge. Sure, I could bark out credits to get more and better stage opportunities, but I know those opportunities await me regardless. I get more out of seeing how long it takes me to show and prove my worth.

The comics are cool, although they like to roast a lot more than I do. And they're good at it too, especially Baldhead Phillips. Vince Acevedo, who I met in Houston just three days before I moved, has really looked out for me. He put me on a couple of showcases and helped me get booked at the Laugh Factory. Just to name a few others; Brandi Denise, Dave Helem, and Marcos Lara have helped make the Chicago transition a smooth one.

I'll be competing this Wednesday in the Midwest Make It Funny Competition. It will be held at Jokes and Notes, which is one of the premier comedy clubs in the city. It should be fun.

In fact, the whole Chi-town experience should be fun. It's been a bit challenging so far, but that was expected. The fiancé and I are still searching for a home. To make matters worse, my bank account was cleaned out after my wallet was stolen on a trip I took back to Houston last week. But hey, God's got it under control. He's going to work every stumbling block out for the better.

In the meantime, I'll be working on my craft and enjoying life in Chicago.

It's so cold in Chicago that every time I drop my debit card outside I cancel it.

AUGUST 28, 2014

I'M COMPETING in the Midwest Make It Funny Competition tonight. I've made it to the finals and The Crown Is Mine! The question is: how thoroughly am I going to win?

Ronnie George won the contest. The runners up were Hot Sauce from

St. Louis, followed by two Detroit comedians: Josh Adams and Ron Taylor. I was thoroughly beaten.

SEPTEMBER 1, 2014

JUST GOT BACK from the Oddball Comedy Festival. The show featured Bill Burr, Hannibal Burress, Sara Silverman, and more.

The show was amazing! I saw things I've never seen at a comedy show. Hannibal had people juggling during his set. Silverman had one of her bits show up on a Family Feud style screen. Comics came out in jumpsuits with their faces on them. It was great!

The night ended a bit sour though. Sandrell and I got into a heated argument. There was a lot of yelling and cursing going on. Almost all of it came from me.

On the bright side, I have a few showcases coming up that I'm excited about. Next Monday I'm doing the Gotham Comedy Club in New York. The following Friday I'm auditioning for Shaq's All Stars in Dallas, and in October I'm auditioning for a TV show on FOX titled *Laughs*. I've never had three showcases within a month. I hope I nail them all.

Comics, if there is a comedian you really like, do your best to go see him or her live. You'll be inspired and halfway tempted to leave the show early to go work on your craft.

DECEMBER 11, 2014

IT'S BEEN a while since I last wrote an entry because once again I lost my journal. My girl and I moved into our apartment on September 15th and the journal was somehow misplaced in the shuffle.

So I just read my last entry mentioning that I had three upcoming showcases. For various reasons I only ended up doing one of them. That one being the Shaq's All Stars in Dallas, and it wasn't an all-star performance from me.

Tony Rock was in the Windy City for a weekend in October. I was privileged to guest spot on one of his shows at the Chicago Improv. In addition, I did two booked shows at the Laugh Factory courtesy of comedians Jay Washington and Joey Villagomez, and I had feature weekends at both Riddles Comedy Club and Jokes and Notes. That's four out of Chicago's seven comedy clubs I was able to break into.

I was also introduced to a guy by the name of Mikey O. He's Chicago's premier independent comedy promoter, and he services predominantly Latin audiences. He holds most of his shows at Joe's Bar, and he also hosts many private events at schools and churches. I have been fortunate to be booked on several of his shows thus far.

One thing that has been a concern over the past three months has been my memory. I forgot about three shows.

Never has that happened to me before. I'm not sure what caused these brain farts, but it prompted me to buy a planner. It should help keep me organized.

Man, it feels good to write. I've been so down and frustrated as of late. I've been struggling with certain sins and lack of a work ethic. It can get depressing at times. I pray that God carries me through this funk. I'll be glad when my laziness is a distant memory.

Little did I know, I would soon need God to carry me through something far foggier than a little "funk."

15

Sometimes Life Throws a Haymaker

JANUARY 1, 2015

It's a new year, which usually means new hopes and new dreams. that's exactly what it means for me this year. Last year I made ten goals and didn't accomplish a single one, if I were to be honest about it. This year I plan on accomplishing all of my goals. Yep, all one of them.

That's right, I decided this year I will keep my goal simple. That goal is to make it on a NACA showcase. I figure setting one goal should help me center my focus. Anything else that happens this year is a bonus.

FEBRUARY 8, 2015

ON JANUARY 19TH, Martin Luther King Day, Leroy

Williams passed away. A fatal heart attack took the Hypno-bro's life.

Leroy was my mentor. He was the first person to put me on a show at the Houston Improv. He took me on the road. He gave me an opportunity to be a writer for a pilot. I could literally go on and on about how Leroy impacted my young comedy career. He's had the most influence on it so far.

This past Wednesday, Sandrell and I flew into Houston for a benefit show that we helped plan for him. It turned out nicely and was one of the best shows I've ever been a part of. I hosted the event and many of Leroy's old comedy pals took the stage to pay tribute to him.

It's almost been three weeks since he passed, and it's still hard to fathom. You just don't expect to befriend someone and then lose them just six years later. Leroy always supported me, and he always rooted for me. He always had sound advice for me even when I was a beginner. A lot of the vets don't pay the newbies any attention. Leroy always did.

Leroy did so much for me. He was a giving man. I could never repay him, but I didn't have to. He only asked of me that I pay it forward. And I promise that's what I'll do.

I spoke with Leroy very briefly the week before he passed. Until now, I hadn't given the conversation deep thought. I now remember that even his last words to me were a vote of encouragement. Those words were:

"Mickey, have a great set."

When Sandrell informed Leroy a few months earlier that our upcoming wedding was set for February 21ˢᵗ, he was disappointed as he had a show that day and wouldn't be able to attend. Ironically, his funeral was held on the same day.

APRIL 1, 2015

TO SAY a lot has happened since I last wrote in this journal would be an understatement. Most of the events were dope.

For starters, I got married to my girlfriend of the last four years. Yep February 21st is the day that Sandrell and I became one. It was a beautiful wedding in which I must thank both of our mothers for their work to make sure it turned out awesome! I was also honored to have Houston's Hottest Karaoke DJ, Lady BG, handle the music for the event.

That following Tuesday we returned to Chicago from Texas and I started a new job working at the same place where Sandrell works. It's been a blessing as extra income is often a good thing.

Three weeks later I was back in Houston for the 6th edition of my MickeyLodeon birthday party. I brought Willie Lynch Jr. to headline and it turned out great—the best one since MickeyLodeon 2. When I returned to Chicago I started co-producing Pilsen Stand-up, a monthly comedy show with comedians Jaime De Leon and Abi Sanchez.

On another dope note, I recently signed with Neon Entertainment. It's a booking agency that will be handling all my college gigs. I spent two weeks at the top of the year emailing agencies various clips of my standup along with a nice headshot and resume. I emailed every agency I came across online and within two months Neon follow up with an offer. I was ecstatic.

This could be huge for me!

My wife is happy because I'm starting to do more handiwork around the house. Yesterday I picked up a nail that I saw on the ground. And instead of throwing it away, I glued it back on her finger. #relationshipgoals

AUG 12, 2015

ON THE MORNING of August 10, 2015 just a few minutes after midnight, I was dealt a devastating blow. It was perhaps the darkest moment of my life to date.

On that morning, Dejuan Jamal Housley left his earthly body to be with the Heavenly Father. He passed away due to complications from heatstroke he had suffered just the day before.

I haven't cried much since Dejuan's passing and I don't

completely understand why. Maybe it's because I know he's in a far better place. Maybe it's the prayers from friends and family that keep me sustained. Or maybe it just doesn't feel real.

It's difficult to fathom little Mel growing up without her father. It's hard to believe there's no more friendly-some-times-turned-serious-brotherly-competition with him. And it's tough to imagine all the laughs that are left on the table with his departure.

Sure, I'm the comedian by profession, but Dejuan was funnier. His antics were hysterical.

The way he would imitate Mariah's inability to dance. Or seeing the look on our poor cat's face when Dejuan would dry hump him. How he relentlessly clowned me for once thinking it was an honor to look like the former NBA player Sam Cassell (look him up). How he would greet my wife with a ridiculous bow because she was part Asian. How he would drive and simulate himself getting shot and killed at red lights.

FOR THE SECOND time I took an extended break from writing. The first time was because I lost a notebook. This time was because I lost a brother. I didn't finish the entry I began writing about Dejuan though my intention was to do so. Whenever I had the mind to write about something significant, I failed to proceed because I hadn't finished the entry on Dejuan. I know I could have simply finished Dejuan's entry and carried on with the next, but I couldn't bring myself to do it. As more time passed, it became more difficult for me, mentally at least, to write anything. Eventually, I just disregarded writing altogether. Another two years would fly by before I applied pen to paper once more. Therefore, once again, I must fill in the gaps.

AUGUST 12, 2015 – Dejuan Continued (September 23, 2017)

I NEVER FINISHED WRITING this entry and I hate that I didn't. It would have easily been my longest one as I had a lot on my heart. I remember that I thought I would pick back up after flying home to Chicago, but I never did. Needless to say, I missed my brother terribly, and I still do.

Dejuan and I were close—only fourteen months separated us in age. He was the best man at my wedding (he was my replacement best man, but still). I was the last family member to see him alive despite living the farthest away. I was in Houston for a show the week before he passed. I paid him a visit and just seven days later he was gone.

Thinking of Dejuan sometimes helps me get out of a funk. He had big dreams for me as a comedian and I want to continue to work hard, not just for me now but for his daughter Melanie. I must make sure my Niecy Pooh is straight.

My brother's example continues to help me on a spiritual level too. Dejuan really rededicated himself to Christ his last year on earth. Sometimes my beliefs get rattled by all the attacks I see on Facebook towards Christians. It's one thing to disagree, but don't disrespect.

It's been two years now since Dejuan departed, yet the family thinks of him daily, especially my mom. She previously told us on several occasions that one of her biggest fears was to bury a child. Sadly, she had to live out that fear —her worst nightmare. Although just writing this small portion is beginning to tear me up, I'm glad I came back to this entry and was able to somewhat complete it.

R.I.P. Dejuan. I pray the world knows how dope you were.

16

Paranoid, Thrilled, and Dejected

<u>**SEPTEMBER 9, 2015**</u>

FOR KEN'S thirtieth birthday he threw a big show at the Houston Improv, and featured a dope lineup that included me along with Leonard Outz and Willie Lynch Jr.

This was perhaps my first significant show since burying my brother just two weeks prior. I sold roughly forty tickets for the show. I was ready.

Except I wasn't ready—Not in the least bit.

In the weeks leading up to the show, I found myself caught up in YouTube videos claiming that a meteor was going to hit Earth on Sept 23rd, 2015. I began to believe that the world was going to end. I also believed that the Rapture would either proceed or occur shortly after following this massive strike on Earth. Clearly, I was becoming increasingly paranoid, and I wanted to make sure I was living a godly life. I didn't want to let Sandrell know how I felt, making her potentially as stressed as me.

I convinced myself that I had to warn the audience at Ken's show. I spent my days trying to form a way to get this message across while still being funny. When it came time for the show I didn't do a good job of either. I was hardly funny and barely said anything about the world ending.

It was an embarrassing performance. I had people that came to see me for the first time, and I felt like I wasted their time and money. My brother Denzell said a woman at the table next to him loudly complained to her friends that I wasn't funny. Sometime later Willie Lynch opined to me that Ken made a mistake by having me follow him on the show.

Mariah suspected something was off about me that night. She knew her big brother was capable of a far better show than what I demonstrated. She thought, however, it had more to do with Dejuan's recent passing. When I shared with her what was going on in my head that night she expressed some regret that she didn't find out in advance of the show. She would've tried to reassure me.

As September 23rd drew near, I was still quite shaken up about the upcoming doom that I perceived to be certain. Even if a meteor was not to strike, I guessed the government may unleash a massive bomb on us unsuspecting civilians. Obviously, I was a mental mess in need of some advice, and there was only one person I could think of to help me.

When Stacy Anderson first began doing comedy, she often

spoke of a DVD she watched that almost caused her to lose her mind, literally. I called Stacy and shared with her what I was going through. She quickly reminded me that no one can put a date on when this world will end. Only the Lord knows. She also suggested that I focus more on what the Bible is saying about this earth than what YouTube is saying.

The talk with Stacy helped tremendously. From then on, I refused to entertain the YouTube prophets. Additionally, I very recently read a book called *Saved Without a Doubt* by John MacArthur, that has helped.

Trying to act holy after living a life full of lust and sin isn't going to make me feel any safer in the face of impending doom. Jesus was crucified for a good cause. While I am expected to live a life of righteousness, it's His blood that covers me when I fail. And it's not hard to tell that I fail often.

It goes without saying that the meteor expected to bomb Earth in late September was a no call, no show. The only bomb that took place was me on the Improv stage. Good thing it's not on YouTube.

> And the peace of God, which transcends all
> understanding, will guard your hearts
> and your minds in Christ Jesus. ~
>
> Philippians 4:7

OCTOBER 23, 2015

AFTER SIGNING on with Neon Entertainment earlier in the year it was time to get the ball rolling with the college gigs. The first step was a showcase at the APCA Midwest Regional in Iowa.

APCA is one of the two major corporations that allow artists of all genres to showcase in front of students and representatives of Universities across the nation. APCA is the smaller of the two companies and easier to showcase for.

NACA is the larger company. It's tougher to score a showcase with NACA, but it exposes you to more schools with potentially larger budgets. For now, I was more than happy to be showcasing with APCA. I did well enough to book a few schools. I surely thought I would've scored more gigs, and was a tad disappointed with myself, but on the bright side, it was more than I would've had if I didn't do the showcase. Complaints aside, it was a nice experience.

DECEMBER 12, 2015

WELL THIS WAS A PRETTY significant day for my family. My parents have four children together: me, Dejuan, Denzell, and Mariah in that order. (We also have an older brother, Dion, who my dad had prior to meeting my mother.)

While the older boys opted not to go to college upon finishing high school, Denzell enrolled at St. Edwards University in Austin, TX. This was an odd choice considering this school did not have a football program. Denzell had a pretty good high school career at the defensive end position. In any case, Denzell would only study at St. Edwards for a year before returning home.

Mariah, on the other hand, enrolled at Texas State University, maybe a half hour from where Denzell attended school. Unlike her brothers, she would go the distance.

I don't think anyone should ever underestimate the commitment and sacrifice it takes to complete college. Everyone was so proud of Mariah. I only wished Dejuan could've been there.

I know he was proud too.

JANUARY 31, 2016

I HAD A COLLEGE BOOKING AGENT, and this was the weekend I really began to gush about having this service. This was also the weekend I began to fear I had already jeopardized it.

The founder of Neon Entertainment, Scott Talrico, informed me that he had four colleges for me to work in a span of four days, in three states. This was wonderful news, but it was a weird weekend in which Sandrell was with me at my first show, not with me at the second show, and then forced to be with me at the third and fourth shows.

The first show was in Buffalo, NY at Niagara University. Because my agency is based in Buffalo, Scott made his way over to the show. His presence made me nervous. I was forgetting jokes and it appeared as if I didn't have enough material to finish the show—not exactly the impression you want to present to your agent when it's his first time seeing you live.

After Buffalo, I left for West Virginia where the show went much better. It was fun because I was performing at a college, but it felt like I was performing at a nice bar. Perhaps that's because I was performing at a nice bar. Wheeling Jesuit University has a bar on campus. And they aren't just serving apple juice and tea either. It's the real deal. It was one of the best shows I've ever done.

For reasons I can't remember Sandrell had to fly back to Chicago after the Buffalo show. For reasons I do remember she had to meet me in the middle of nowhere.

Because I don't have a driver's license, I cannot rent a car under my own name. This made getting to Binghamton, NY for my next show quite tricky. The plan was to bum a ride from one of the students at Wheeling Jesuit to nearby Pittsburg, PA. From Pittsburg I would then fly to New York. It was a plan I assured my worried wife would work. And it would have if I had asked more than just two students for a ride. No worries, I thought—I'll just take an Uber to Pittsburg. This surely would've worked if Uber existed in Wheeling, WV.

The next day I found some sort of shuttle service that could get me to Pittsburg. However, the shuttle wouldn't get me to Pittsburg in time to catch the plane that would get me to New York in time for my show. Sandrell, meanwhile, rented a car in Chicago and drove hours to my rescue. When I got to Pittsburg, I ordered an Uber and convinced the driver to travel 2 hours to some tiny town where I would meet up with Sandrell.

I was relieved when I caught up with her, but by the time that happened, there was no way I was making it to New York in time for the show. I had to call and cancel the show. I was embarrassed, and I feared that I had severely damaged my reputation and reliability with the agency. Thankfully, that wasn't the case.

The last show was at Edinboro University in Erie, PA. It went smoothly and also served as my big pay day. When the smoke cleared, I returned home making $4000 for the weekend. If I could earn that every weekend, I'd be able to do some absurd things.

Like rent a car with no license.

MARCH 13, 2016

ANOTHER YEAR, another dope birthday show. It was MickeyLodeon 7 this year and I had a blend of comedians from all over the place.

Ms. CuttnUp from Milwaukee. Owen Dunn from Houston. Bryson Brown from Austin. Jay Washington, Michael Isaac, and my headliner, Vince Acevedo, from Chicago. Every one of them had a great set on the show!

The show was a success. The feedback I received was that the show overall was better than the year before, which was nice to hear.

JUNE 24, 2016

IN CHICAGO, I found myself a part of a standup comedy group just as I had been in Houston with the Maks of Comedy. My group this time, was a quintet comprised of me, Vince Acevedo, Lucky Luciano, Manny Acosta, and Steve Rinaldi—better known as 5 the Hard Way.

Our first show was on March 12th in Indiana and produced by Tom Byelick. The look and feel we wanted to portray was that of the Rat Pack. I think we pulled it off. We all performed in suits and true to form had a token black guy. (I'll let you guess who that was.) The Indiana show was nice, and it served as a prelude to a bigger show to come.

On June 24th, we had two sold out shows at Joe's on Weed St., which we had promoted for months. The buildup was great. We had a photo shoot and used one of the pictures to make a nice flyer. Our suits were picked out and ready to go, and with the help of Sandrell, we shot a video that we played before the show. The DJ played songs by the Rat Pack as each performer made his way to the stage.

All of us had awesome sets that night. I personally enjoyed the first show more. My set on that show was magical. I'd hang it in my top three, for sure. The crowd was fired up for both shows, and it was purely electric. I'm not exaggerating in the least bit when I say we were received like rock stars!

So, there it is—two highly successful shows. It sounds like one of my most memorable nights as a comedian, right? However, if it sounds like one of my best nights in comedy then it's safe to assume that it may have been one of my worst as well.

You see my night wasn't over yet. I had one more show to do—an audition at Jokes and Notes the night before it closed. The audition was for TBS and talent scout Tamera Goins. Tamera is most recognized in comedy circles as the lead booker for the Shaq's All Stars of Comedy. I had auditioned for her before in Dallas. I didn't do too hot that night.

I got another crack at her the first year I moved to Chicago. I fared better than my Dallas showcase, but when speaking to her after the show she made a remark, which served as motivation.

"I don't remember you from Dallas," she said. "And if I don't remember you then you're not writing enough."

I was determined to show her I was for real on this third try. I was bound to crack her this time. However, the only thing I ended up cracking was my confidence.

Mind you, having an earlier engagement caused me to be significantly late to this audition. When I got to Jokes and

Notes (literally minutes before taking the stage), I began my set and—BOOM!

After just having perhaps the best set I'd ever had a few hours before, I was now having the absolute worst set of my life. At a contest, in front of the woman that I vowed I would make eat her words. I bombed—badly. *Nobody* laughed at my jokes. Maybe one or two people, tops. When my time was up, I walked off stage and went straight to my car, heading for home in less than two minutes. I'd never went home after a set so fast in my life.

Before I could get to my car, I heard a voice call after me.

"Mickey! How did it go?" Mary, the owner of the Jokes and Notes asked.

"It was okay," I told her. "Could've been a little better."

I lied. It could've been a lot better.

As I mentioned, the legendary comedy club was closing the next day. It was tempting to stay at home licking my wounds. Instead, I made my way back over to the club to help celebrate Mary and her amazing contributions to comedy as an African American, female, comedy club owner. She awarded me plenty of showcases and opportunities since moving to Chicago. I am forever grateful to her for that.

While at Mary's celebration, I learned that right before I performed the previous night (the set that totally bombed), a young female comedian took her panties off onstage. From then on none of the comedians did well apparently.

"You weren't the only one that bombed," said comedian T-Murph.

That certainly helped my fractured ego, but not by much. I hate to admit it, but that show almost fully convinced me that I couldn't make black people laugh anymore. For the next year I would rarely perform at the black rooms. Fear wasn't the only factor that played into that, but it was the leading factor, no doubt.

I will never forget June 24ᵗʰ—the night I experience a great high only to be quickly sabotaged by a greater low.

Bad sets aren't created equal. Some are tougher to deal with than others. I get why people refuse to speak in front of audiences—to avoid moments of failure and embarrassment. My bombing at the showcase was a dark moment for me. Fortunately, there was a beaming light at the end of the tunnel. One I had been waiting on for a long time.

17

It's Showtime!

SEPTEMBER 11, 2016

IT WAS a great weekend for me. For the first time since moving to Chicago, my family came to visit me.

My mom along with Denzell, Mariah, and Jude flew up to Chi-Town.

Not to be left behind, Grandma Beulah made her way to the Windy City as well. At eighty years old, it was her first time getting on a plane and she loved it.

Family is important to me, and I always enjoy being around mine.

We didn't do a whole lot, but I did take them to play Whirly Ball, which I recommend doing if you're ever in Chicago.

SEPTEMBER 18, 2016

FOR THE FIRST time in three years I took part in the NBC StandUp Showcase. Every summer representatives of NBC select four cities to travel to in search of talent. One hundred comedians line up outside the comedy club early Saturday morning for a one-minute showcase.

The NBC reps then pick thirty comics, give or take, to come back in the afternoon for a two-minute round. From there ten comics will be called to showcase the next night in front of a live audience. Lastly, two comedians are selected to fly to L.A. for the finals where they will compete against the comedians that were selected in the other cities.

Nashville was the last city of the year for NBC. I came really close to not going. The fact that I worked a 9 to 5 was complicating my decision. Nashville is an eight-hour drive from Chicago. If I advanced to the Sunday show, I'd have to leave immediately after to make it to work by 7:00 a.m. Sandrell slapped me and reminded me that my goal was to be a comedian, not a shipping clerk. To Nashville we went.

In four tries I had never made it to the Sunday showcase. I really wanted to get there this year. So I prayed. I asked that God take me to the Sunday showcase and that's exactly what happened.

I blazed through the one-minute round, having arguably the best set of my group. My two-minutes wasn't as hot, but it got the job done.

Sandrell and I were ecstatic to learn that I had made it to the Sunday showcase. And to think that I almost didn't make the trip.

Sunday morning, we went to a bar so I could watch the Houston Texans play. As we were searching for a seat, I heard my name called. To my pleasant surprise, it was the NBC reps. They were there watching the New York Giants play. Here we were kicking it with NBC reps, one of whom books the comedians for The Tonight Show.

Evening rolled around, and it was time for the showcase. It was at the Zanies Comedy Club. My brunch with the reps didn't help me much, not that I expected it to. I had an okay set. Not my best, not my worst. There were some guys that were hitting it, and deservingly moved on to the big showcase in L.A.

In the end, I felt pretty good having advanced further than I ever had in the NBC StandUp. I almost wished I would've prayed to make it to L.A.

NOVEMBER 16, 2016

THE COMEDY BAR was a Chicago club that took me some time to break into. After doing a few guest spots, Sahar, the general manager, hit me with a pretty cool offer.

They were starting a new show at the club and they wanted me to be the host. This was dope. I'd be a regular host at a comedy club. On November 16th, I hosted Movie-oke night at the Comedy Bar.

Movie-oke was a concept that combined movies and karaoke. People were afforded the opportunity to go on stage and perform a movie scene while it played on a giant screen. Being the karaoke fiend that I am, I assumed this would be a great event to host every Wednesday.

The first night went well. There were some kinks we worked out that helped for a bit, but before long movie-oke night began going downhill. It was hard to get a consistent crowd in every week, and while I love Karaoke, I'm not really a movie guy.

I rarely watch a movie more than once, deeming it a waste of time. Therefore, it's hard for me to recall a movie scene even with the words displayed on a screen.

After a few months, Sahar informed me that they would take a short break from movie-oke.

The break has lasted a year now. I have no complaints.

DECEMBER 3, 2016

MY DEAR FRIEND and fellow comedian Mona Abur-mishan had a friend in Dearborn, MI who produced an annual comedy festival. I hadn't done a festival in two years. I vowed to stop doing them unless it was the Boston Comedy Festival or the Montreal Comedy Festival.

All the other festivals are pretty much in their infancy stages, no older than five or six years. You burn money to sign up with no guarantee you'll get selected, nor is there a refund if you aren't. You must fund your own travel and there's not enough industry people attending these festivals to make them worth going to.

Despite these factors, when Mona asked me if I wanted in, I said, "yes." I mean, I didn't have to sign up, and being just a few hours away I didn't have to burn cash on a plane ticket.

The Dearborn Comedy Festival is quite possibly the best one I've done so far. The creator, Amer Zahr, to my surprise, compensated me for my drive. A nice hotel was provided, which was also surprising considering you usually take care of your own lodging at comedy festivals. Where most festivals have upwards of forty comedians performing, this was just a tight group of fifteen.

Amer is an Arab comedian and Dearborn is highly populated by Arab people. The festival reflected that as the audience was mostly Arab and so were about half of the comedians that performed.

Another cool thing about this festival was that some of my family drove from Flint, MI to catch me perform. And peep this. They came on just a day's notice.

I had such a great time that I became once again intrigued with the idea of performing at comedy festivals. I would later do an unprecedented three comedy festivals in one week, earning the moniker Mr. Festival.

JANUARY 22, 2017

ALI WAS in town headlining at Zanies Comedy Club. Zanies is the lone comedy club in Chicago that I've yet to be booked at. So I was glad when Ali managed to get me a guest spot on the Sunday show.

After the show, Ali, Netra Babin (who had recently moved to Chicago), and I were planning to find somewhere to eat. However, I received a text that forced me to alter my plans. It was Sandrell stating that she wasn't feeling well, and I needed to come home immediately.

Not long after I got home I found myself in the Emergency Room with my wife. This made the second time in a week.

Coming home from work a few days prior, she complained of having chest pains and numbness in her arms while also experiencing shortness of breath and light headedness. With all this going on, she feared she was having a heart attack and urged that I take her to the hospital. After running a few tests, it appeared to the doctors that everything checked out and she was fine.

Now here we were again at the hospital. After the doctors again confirmed that nothing was wrong with her body, they suspected that she was possibly suffering from anxiety attacks. Apparently, she worries too much, especially when I'm out late. Somehow, she found a way to make her body shut down if I don't come home at a decent time. Women, I tell ya.

On the bright side, knowing what was plaguing her body

helped Sandrell to calm down when she felt worried or stressed. She hasn't had any anxiety attacks since. Well, until she ate a weed cookie one day at a party.

But that's another story.

MARCH 12, 2017

JUST OVER TWO hundred people flocked to the Joke Joint Comedy Showcase for MickeyLodeon 8. It was a nearly sold out show and by far my best turn out since I began producing the show.

The show was dope from start to finish. The opening comedians collectively did well. Mike Worm, Boogie, Sandrell, Rob Young and Tim Mathis all blessed the stage. My feature comedian Justin Thompson from Beaumont, TX was awesome. My headliner was Brian "Da Wildcat" Smith from Chicago. In my opinion, he's the funniest comedian in Chi-Town and his performance was simply amazing. The crowd was with him from the moment he stepped on stage. They even stuck with him as he dogged Houston's beloved Frenchy's Chicken.

At the end of the show and after nearly every ounce of laughter was extracted from the room, I gave away some gifts as I do every year. Usually it's fruit baskets and gift cards. This year I was able to include two free massages courtesy of Denzell who was the manager at a Massage Envy near the Galleria.

This was truly a fun show. MickeyLodeon 2 had served as my personal favorite for six years strong. I was finally able to declare with confidence that MickeyLodeon 8 now had the top spot. With a great turnout and a hot lineup, it raised the bar for MickeyLodeons to come. It was the best birthday show a thirty-year-old man could hope for.

MARCH 26, 2017

LAST NIGHT I was out catching a comedy show produced by a pair of locals in Chicago. I would've been performing on a show of my own had it not been cancelled a few days prior. The cancellation of the show caused me to miss out on two other shows that wanted my services on that same day.

So rather than perform, I spent my Saturday night as a spectator of a well ran comedy show on the south side of Chicago. For a combination of reasons, I became very depressed as I left the show. I sat in my car and repeatedly questioned, cursed, and doubted myself. I had just made it eight years as a comedian and wasn't feeling confident about the direction of my career. I feared that I was becoming a bitter comic. They're everywhere. Twenty-five year veterans upset at how their careers panned out as they watch their peers shine across the TV screens.

I didn't have to be famous, but I for damn sure wanted a national television appearance. At least one. Call me insecure if you will, but I needed that validation. It's been a goal of mine for years, and I always perceived it to be a foregone conclusion.

I've done a countless number of shows. I have people tell me I'm funny. Talented. A rising star. Well, why don't the TV executives feel this way? What am I doing wrong? Am I not as funny as people tell me I am? Am I even supposed to be a comedian?

These were questions I posed to myself, but I didn't stop there. I prayed and posed the same questions to God as well. A selfish prayer I'm sure.

Perhaps my selfishness was answered the next day when I received an email stating that FOX was looking for some comedians to submit for an opportunity to perform on *Showtime at the Apollo*. You would think I'd be thrilled, but I wasn't. The Apollo has a reputation for booing artists if they deem a performance to be lackluster. Nevertheless, I submitted my video and headshot.

Within a few days I learned that the producers liked my video and wanted to set up a Skype interview to further determine if I would be a good fit for the show. This was the closest I had ever been to a national television opportunity, yet I was still unsatisfied. I don't want my first appearance to be on an amateur showcase. I was eight years in and no amateur. I was being picky and prideful. The nerve!

I proceeded to do the Skype interview convincing myself that this could lead to opportunities without the word "amateur" attached to them. A young talent scout by the name of Torriel Simon conducted my interview. She was nice and coached me through the process. There were some issues with the Skype connection and screen resolution, but we muscled through it.

The interview ended and Sandrell confirmed my belief that it went well. Could it have been better? No doubt about it. But there was nothing else I could do but wait. By now I realized that I did want to do *Showtime at the Apollo*. I made a vow to myself that I wouldn't have a beer until I got the confirmation to do Apollo.

A week later, I was gladly drinking beers again. That's how long it took for me to give up on Apollo. They had begun casting comedians for the show, and I figured I had missed out on yet another opportunity.

Oh well. At least I wasn't depressed.

MAY 26, 2017

TWO MONTHS HAD PASSED since I did my Skype interview for *Showtime at the Apollo*. I hadn't heard anything and assumed I missed out. That was until I received an unexpected email from Victoria, one of the talent scouts for the show.

She informed me that the producers did in fact like me, but the quality of the Skype interview was not good. According to her, the producers wanted to set up another interview and advised that I find a place with a strong internet connection and good lighting. Basically, they didn't want me conducting the second interview from home. (That reminds me, I need to buy some more light bulbs).

I chose the famous Second City Theater to conduct my second attempt at the interview. The interview was once again with Torriel. We still had some troubles with the internet connection, but the lighting was much improved. Torriel coached me once more reminding me that it was important to display a lot of energy and personality.

Some of the questions asked were:

"How long have you been performing standup comedy?" Eight years.

"Which comedians influence you most?" Dave Chappelle, D.L. Hughley.

"What would it mean to appear on *Showtime at the Apollo*?" Great! I grew up watching the show. It'd be an honor.

I felt a lot better about my chances of being selected after the second interview. A couple of days later I was notified that I indeed had been selected for *Showtime at the Apollo*. A week later I was on a plane to New York.

The quick turn of events caught me by surprise. I was forced to cancel two shows, one of which caused some controversy. It's never fun cancelling a show, but neither is compromising the biggest opportunity of your career.

With the bulk of the preliminary necessities out of the way, it became clear. I was finally going to perform on TV and it felt good!

BEFORE I GO, I leave behind one final entry. It's arguably the most important one. Without it this book likely doesn't get published. After another long drought of no entries, and with a bunch of free time on my hands, I suddenly had the urge to write. And so, I did.

With that said, it was a pleasure sharing my first eight years of standup with you as well as my journey to your television screen. I hope that you found it enjoyable. If you are a young comedian, I hope that you're able to avoid some of the mistakes that I've shared and that this journal inspires you to chronicle your journey as well.

Pray (or meditate) before every show and practice your craft every day!

JUNE 2, 2017

FOR THE FIRST six-and-a-half years of my comedy career, I wrote a journal chronicling my experience in the business —the highs, the lows, and the in betweens. I wrote sometimes consistently and other times sporadically.

The past year and a half, I got away from writing for one reason or another. It could've been that I lost a notebook or two. Lack of free time while working a 9 to 5 could've played a part. Or perhaps I simply got discouraged.

Whatever the case was, at this present moment it doesn't matter. For at this very moment I write. I'm not sure if this is the only entry for years to come, or the first of many more. What I do know is something pressed me to write. Just a few moments ago, I was reminded of something.

I initially started writing this journal in February of 2009, just a couple of weeks before I would perform standup for the first time. At some point, I decided I would publish this journal. I felt like it would be a good read—the detailed journey of an up and coming comedian. The goal was to publish part 1 of the journal when I made my first TV appearance. The problem? It took longer than anticipated, hence the aforementioned discouragement.

I estimated it would take five years tops to make it on TV. It's been eight. But the good news is that I *am* making my first TV appearance. In fact, I'm about thirty-six hours from my big opportunity. That's right, thirty-six hours from taping for *Showtime at the Apollo*.

It's kind of a dream come true when I think about it. I've been trying not to get too thrilled, but to be on a show you watched as a child is rather cool. To be called on stage by Steve Harvey, the man I watched host the show for many years is cool too. My brothers and I used to catch the belt trying to watch the show. My mom would come home from work late expecting us to be in bed, only to find us in front of the TV booing singers and dancing like the Sandman.

I was flown from Chicago to New York where I've been staying for the past week at the Stewart Hotel. It's a decent Hotel that sits kitty-corner to Madison Square Garden. I told my family about my taping right before I left Chicago, and they're all overjoyed for me. But none more so than my wife, whose probably far more excited than I am. She's so stoked that she bought a plane ticket to see the show Saturday, even though she has to perform in a stage play the same night.

It feels good to make my family proud, especially my mom. I know she's extremely happy for me, and it's comforting to know that she's always praying for me.

Of course, this opportunity would be more special if Dejuan were here to share it with. I can hardly fathom that my brother won't get to see me grace national television—at least not here on Earth anyways. I mean this guy was with me every step of the way, from my first time ever stepping onto a comedy stage to road gigs and on and on. I know he's watching from Heaven.

As for everyone else, myself included, we'll watch whenever the season airs. I thank God so much for such an opportunity. Best case scenario is that this jump starts an abundance of more opportunities. One can only wait and see.

Which reminds me, even though it doesn't look as if I'll be publishing this journal by the time *Showtime at the Apollo* airs, the gig served as a gentle kick in the butt. It reminded me to keep writing because we truly never know where our thoughts, words, and emotions may take us.

One can only wait and see!

A few weeks after I taped "Showtime at the Apollo," I quit my job to pursue standup comedy full-time. It was the third and last time I made such a move.

About the Author

Mickey Housley is a professional comedian who travels the country performing at colleges and comedy clubs alike. His seamless blend of animation and wit has been featured on FOX, Comcast and ComedyTyme TV. Mickey currently resides in Chicago, IL where he co-produces Pilsen Stand-up every third Wednesday of the month. He's also the house emcee at the House of Blues for the Tuesday night comedy show, which is a tourist attraction where many come from all over and are treated to an endless night of laughter.

www.mickey-housley.com

Made in the USA
Lexington, KY
19 July 2018